PRAISE FOR *ECHOES FROM THE HILLTOP*

"*Echoes from the Hilltop* is a must-read for anyone who is associated with Maryville College. The story of Margaret Henry not only provides inspiration but also illustrates the continuity from the early twentieth century to our current time in the twenty-first century in both the institutional mission and the way that generous support from donors is translated into student success. . . . I am forever grateful for Miss Margaret's work, and I am grateful to Polly Bowers for ensuring that her story continues to be celebrated as an inspiration and a challenge."

—*Dr. Tom Bogart, President, Maryville College*

"*Echoes from the Hilltop* is a welcome addition to the history of Maryville College. Ms. Bowers introduces her readers to Margaret Eliza Henry, a truly remarkable woman who played a critical role during a pivotal time in the life of the college. . . . Margaret Henry's life is a testament to her deep devotion to Maryville College, the mountains in which she was born and raised, and the people who live in them."

—*Paul Threadgill, Professor of Biology, Maryville College*

"Margaret Henry's fund-raising work on behalf of deserving students in the Smoky Mountains has left us with an intimate record of life in Southern Appalachia. Her letters to donors in the north relate oftentimes-overlooked details of private lives in the mountains. We can but hope that her intercessions on behalf of these mountain people helped in some way to prepare them for the changes that were hurtling their way. Not only has Paula Cox Bowers written a biography of a compassionate champion of education, but her judicious selection of Henry's correspondence provides yet one more layer in our understanding of this region at a time of monumental change."

—*Michael Aday, Librarian-Archivist,*
Great Smoky Mountains National Park

"As a development professional and native Maryvillian, I thoroughly enjoyed learning more about Margaret Henry and the communities she served. Her depictions of the college, the mountains, and the mountain people are vivid, loving, and hopeful. Though times and communication have changed drastically, so much remains the same. Maryville College is still dedicated to the education and advancement of its students, and we are ever grateful for the example and hard work of Margaret Henry."

—Suzy Booker, Vice President for Institutional Advancement, Maryville College

"*Echoes from the Hilltop* is a carefully researched work and a worthy tribute to Margaret Henry's love and devotion to obtain hundreds of scholarships for Southern Appalachian students."

—Dr. Shirley Carr Clowney, historian and community activist

"In *Echoes from the Hilltop*, Paula Cox Bowers introduces readers to the unforgettable Margaret Henry, whose indomitable spirit enriched the lives of hundreds of students from the mountains and—through them—thousands of others."

—Millie Sieber, storyteller and alumna, Class of 1958

"If you believe that education changes lives, you will revel in the story of Margaret Henry. Her efforts transformed the lives of many Appalachian adolescents. Her story is a lasting legacy of community service, and it is a tribute to the impact Maryville College has had for nearly two hundred years."

—Sarah DeYoung, retired administrator, University of Tennessee

"This work bears witness to altruism that spans generations. Polly Bowers has salvaged an inspiration that was almost lost to history, and she unveils Miss Henry's character with a nuanced appreciation for Maryville College's spirit, one that showcases how a single life can help so many more. It is a work that will encourage its readers to follow Isaac Anderson's model of doing good on the largest possible scale."

—*Sherilyn Smith, writer*

"Polly Bowers has done a masterful job of compiling a fascinating account of the life and work of Margaret Henry; while her story is a part of Maryville College's history, it also serves as inspiration for its future."

—*Emily Anderson, Senior Minister, New Providence Presbyterian Church, and member, Maryville College Board of Directors*

"For two hundred years Maryville College has had a heart for helping young people, and Margaret Henry, scholarship secretary back when, is a big part of the how and why."

—*Joan Worley, former Director, Lamar Memorial Library, Maryville College (1984–94)*

"If you'd like to be more deeply connected to the people of the Southern Mountains and to the history of Maryville College, you'll want to read this book."

—*Ellie Morrow, retired Vice President for Advancement, Maryville College*

"In *Echoes from the Hilltop*, Paula Cox Bowers uses abundant correspondence from Miss Margaret Henry to paint a picture of a woman whose earnest passion for educating Appalachian young people is still bearing fruit today. Miss Henry's time at Maryville College, as student, dormitory matron, teacher, and finally scholarship secretary until her death in 1916, included crucial years for the college. This book creates a vivid picture of the educational needs of the area and of the donors who supplied those needs through Miss Henry's untiring schedule of travel, speaking, and corresponding."

—*Brennan LeQuire, Reference Librarian, Blount County Public Library*

"This book is surely a treasure for anyone associated with Maryville College, past or present, and to all who have grown up, or now live, in this area."

—*Jorgine Brause, author*

"What a delightful book! You have shown us that Margaret Henry is certainly a 'Heroine of the Southern Mountaineers' and Maryville College."

—*William B. Miller, retired Assistant Superintendent, Blount County Schools*

"Reading *Echoes from the Hilltop* reinforced my pride in my college. Margaret Henry was a strong woman, and Maryville College was secure enough to promote a woman in a man's world."

—*Elizabeth Walton Blackburn, alumna, Class of 1958*

"This book illustrates that Margaret Eliza Henry was much more than a scholarship secretary for Maryville College. She was a youth advocate, social worker, teacher, community organizer, public speaker, and stewardship manager. . . . She exemplified the words of Maryville College's founder, Isaac Anderson: 'Do good on the largest possible scale.'"

—Angela Miller, Director of Alumni Affairs and Stewardship, Maryville College

"Margaret Henry is, indeed, a Maryville College heroine who implemented the vision of Isaac Anderson to offer a college education to those on the frontier, who impacted hundreds of students' lives during her time as scholarship secretary, and who has impacted thousands of students' lives by starting the Scholarship Fund that is today's Maryville Fund."

—Dan Greaser, alumnus and retired member, Maryville College Board of Directors

"*Echoes from the Hilltop* is, quite simply, one of the finest local history books I have read. As Paula Bowers tells us the fascinating story of this remarkable woman, Margaret Eliza Henry, she also captures and presents the old East Tennessee mountain culture; brings to life so many of the students Henry helped, persons otherwise long-lost to time; and contributes a significant chapter to the written history of Maryville College—so fitting as the college approaches its bicentennial. It is a wonderful book that I will read again."

—David Duggan, Blount County Circuit Judge

Echoes *from the* Hilltop

Margaret Henry—
Heroine of the
Southern Mountaineers

▲▲▲

Paula Cox Bowers

THREE ROOSTERS PRESS

Three Roosters Press
PO Box 475
Friendsville, TN 37737

Cover photo "The Three Sisters" courtesy of the Maryville College Office of Communications.

Ordering Information
Quantity sales. Special discounts are available on quantity purchases by corporations, associations, and others. For details, contact the "Special Sales Department" at the address above.

Orders by US trade bookstores and wholesalers. Please contact BCH: (800) 431-1579 or visit www.bookch.com for details.

Cataloguing-in-publication data
Names: Bowers, Paula Cox, author.
Title: Echoes from the hilltop : Margaret Henry—heroine of the southern mountaineers / Paula Cox Bowers.
Description: Includes bibliographical references and index. | Friendsville, TN : Three Roosters Press, 2018.
Identifiers: ISBN 978-1-7322022-0-7 | LCCN 2018950183
Subjects: LCSH Henry, Margaret. | Maryville College, Maryville, Tenn. | Maryville College—History. | Women—Tennessee—Biography. | Women—Tennessee—History. | Tennessee—Biography. | BISAC BIOGRAPHY & AUTOBIOGRAPHY / Women | BIOGRAPHY & AUTOBIOGRAPHY / Historical
Classification: LCC LD3231.M852 .H46 2018 | DDC 378.768/885/092—dc23

Printed in the United States of America

First Edition
22 21 20 19 18 10 9 8 7 6 5 4 3 2 1

To James Alberto Cox—
survivor, loving father, my educational mentor

Contents

	Foreword	vii
	Introduction	ix
Chapter One	Who Was Margaret Henry?	1
Chapter Two	The Deep-Valley Folk of the Southern Mountains	13
Chapter Three	My Dear Old College	41
Chapter Four	Scholarships for Mountain Boys and Mountain Girls	73
Epilogue	Yesterday, Today, Tomorrow	107
	Acknowledgments	113
	Appendix One: Maryville College Buildings, 1868–1916	115
	Appendix Two: Magnolia Cemetery	117
	Appendix Three: Bettie Jane's Essay, Granny Stinnett's Funeral, Two Reports from the Field, and a Tribute	121
	Appendix Four: Donors	133
	Appendix Five: Biographical Sketch and Funeral Address	137
	Notes	155
	Index	167
	About the Author	173

Foreword

Too often people who were once important in the life of a college get lost in history. Miss Margaret Eliza Henry is one of those people. She is mentioned in only two of the three official histories of Maryville College, and her name is likely unknown to current campus residents. But Paula Cox Bowers has determined that Miss Margaret would not be forgotten at the alma mater the two shared. Just over a century after Margaret's untimely death, Polly has brought her back to life in the pages of this book.

Margaret served during the presidency of Dr. Samuel Tyndale Wilson, who is something of a hero to me. It was Dr. Wilson who recognized her talents and drafted her from her duties as a teacher and a matron of Baldwin Hall to become a peripatetic fund-raiser for the college. In that role, she earned the praise that President Wilson expressed for her in his centennial college history and in the funeral oration that he delivered in 1916, an oration that Polly Bowers includes in its entirety in appendix five in *Echoes from the Hilltop.* "Miss Henry was an alumna of the institution," Dr. Wilson said, "and thoroughly imbued with its spirit."[1]

The same words apply to the author of this book. Readers will recognize at once that Polly feels a profound devotion to Maryville College and to Margaret. With her copious quotes from Samuel Tyndale Wilson and Miss Margaret's abundant correspondence, she provides a full and rich picture of this exceptional servant of the college. Polly's own writing talents contribute as well to that picture, convincing me that she could have been a poet or novelist.

Throughout the book the evidence is plentiful that Margaret was deeply committed to the people of the Appalachian Mountains, where her roots lay. As she traveled to distant regions, she spoke from the heart about Appalachian students and their needs with a persuasive earnestness. Polly Bowers conveys Miss Margaret's effectiveness as an emissary with this quote from a friend: "We did not hear about [the mountain people] but we met them, saw them, talked with them, heard their quaint Southern speech, and felt that we had always known them."[2] The reader of *Echoes from the Hilltop* may well agree with me in observing that Paula Cox Bowers has enabled us, a century after Margaret Henry's death, to meet, see, and talk with this heroine of the southern mountaineers, who in her time at Maryville College surely earned a prominent place in its history.

Gerald W. Gibson
President Emeritus, Maryville College

Introduction

From 1870 until 2001, most of the administrative offices at Maryville College were located in Anderson Hall. Each department had a wire cage (storage room) in the basement to hold old records and correspondence. In anticipation of the renovation of Anderson, these records were placed in boxes and taken to the college's History Room in Fayerweather Hall (Fayerweather Science Hall, renamed Fayerweather Hall in 2001). During Kin Takahashi Week of June 2006, a small group of volunteers was asked by Dori May (a Maryville College Librarian) to begin reading and organizing the letters of Margaret E. Henry, who became the college's first scholarship secretary in 1903. We found beautifully written letters that contained history and information about the college, gave vivid descriptions of the Southern Appalachian Mountains and the people who lived there, and told of friends from the Northeast who faithfully gave money for student scholarships. By the end of Kin Takahashi Week, I was hooked and decided to continue working regularly on Margaret's correspondence. It has been a labor of love, and I have come to know a remarkable Maryville College alumna, teacher, and administrator.

For thirteen years, Margaret Henry enabled hundreds of young people from the Southern Appalachians to obtain an education. After her untimely death in 1916, Clemmie J. Henry, Margaret's cousin, became the second scholarship secretary and continued to expand the endowed scholarship program and provide work-study for students. Clemmie began her work with student scholarships in 1918 and retired thirty-four years later.

My father, James A. Cox, Maryville College class of 1929, received both a scholarship and a loan from Clemmie, which enabled this country farm boy from East Tennessee to obtain an education and have a successful career as an accountant in Philadelphia, Pennsylvania. Correspondence from Clemmie Henry reveals that my father finally repaid the loan in 1945 by using money from his Christmas club savings program. He did not purchase a car until that loan was paid off.

I found many similar stories about former students in Margaret Henry's letters. There is no doubt that she cared deeply for the children of the mountains and valleys of East Tennessee. Now, I want you to meet Margaret.

Here is her story.

Paula (Polly) C. Bowers
Maryville College Class of 1958

Margaret Eliza Henry

When I sit in . . . Voorhees Chapel and see it full of sturdy young lives . . . , I feel glad that I am one of the College workers . . . . I believe that the secret of your service is love of your work.

—Margaret E. Henry

CHAPTER ONE

Who Was Margaret Henry?

In 1873, fall-term classes began on the last Wednesday of August. As fifteen-year-old Sam Wilson entered Anderson Hall that morning for the opening chapel service, his 65-year connection with Maryville College as student, professor, president, and president emeritus began. The students gathered in the chapel on the second floor to hear Dr. Peter Mason Bartlett deliver the opening sermon and declare the beginning of the fifty-fifth year of the college.

Of the more than one hundred students enrolled that fall, about twenty-five were in the College Department. Sam was a senior in the Preparatory Department, which prepared students for college work, and his sister, Mary, was a junior in the College Department. She graduated the next year as the first woman at Maryville College and in the state of Tennessee to receive a baccalaureate degree. Mary and Sam were the children of Rev. and Mrs. David M. Wilson, who in 1847 went to Syria as missionaries by appointment of the Board of Foreign Missions. They served in Homs for fourteen years. During that time, both Mary and Sam were born. Sam was only three when the family returned to the United States in 1861 because of Mrs. Wilson's failing health.

On the small campus, Sam became acquainted with the other students very quickly, including Margaret Eliza Henry, who had entered Maryville the year before. As the years passed, the lives of Sam and Margaret followed an interesting parallel course. Above all, both loved their work at Maryville College and served their alma mater with distinction.

Margaret, born on November 29, 1858, was the daughter of William Jasper Henry, Sr., and Eliza Smith Henry. William was born and raised on the John Henry farm in Blount County where Ellejoy Creek flows into Little River. For generations, Henrys had lived in the mountains of East Tennessee. Margaret shared a bit of family history in a letter to Mrs. John Parsons: "I belong to this Scotch-Irish people of the Southern Mountains myself. My paternal grandmother was born in one of the little log cabins of the mountains in a valley so remote, so lawless, and so neglected, that there was never a day of school or Sabbath service there."[1] Margaret was named for her father's sister Margaret and her mother, Eliza Henry.

Though reared on a farm, William was not interested in farming. Antebellum records indicate that he attended Maryville College around 1852 for a short time. Then he turned to the buying and selling of goods. He was a merchant first in the Ellejoy community and then on Main Street in Maryville, where he worked for his father-in-law, J. Gray Smith, until 1861, when the Civil War began.

William Henry enlisted in the Confederate army and served with the First Tennessee Cavalry, Company K. Near the end of the war, while at home on sick leave, he was captured and taken to Camp Chase, a Union prisoner-of-war camp in Columbus, Ohio. He died there on March 21, 1864, just a few weeks before the end of hostilities.

Eliza Smith Henry, Margaret's mother, came from a very different background. Her parents, J. Gray Smith and Sarah [Sayer] Smith, immigrated to America from England in 1831. J. Gray Smith was an educated, well-read man with many interests. Eleven years after arriving in East Tennessee, he wrote a book: *A Brief Historical, Statistical, and Descriptive Review of East Tennessee, United States of America: Developing Its Immense Agricultural, Mining, and Manufacturing Advantages with Remarks to Emigrants.* The book was printed again in 1974. In that edition, Robert McBride, editor of the *Tennessee Historical Quarterly*, added an introduction that gave an interesting account of the Smith family in both England and America:

> James Gray Smith was born at Manchester, Lancashire, England, on October 6, 1797, one of five children of James Smith, of Dunkinfield, and his wife, Mary Gray, of York, who were married in 1792. J. Gray Smith's sister, Mary, married Robert Moffat, a noted missionary, and their daughter, Mary, became the wife of David Livingstone, the well-known missionary-explorer of Africa. One of Smith's brothers, John, a pastor of Manchester, later went as a missionary to Madras, India, and was lost at sea. . . .
>
> James Gray Smith was married in St. Mary's Church, Manchester, on his 32 birthday, October 6, 1829, to Sarah [Sayer], of London. Soon thereafter, in 1831, they took ship for Philadelphia, Pennsylvania, where Smith was naturalized.
>
> Sarah [Sayer] Smith died in Philadelphia in 1838 and that same year Smith took his four children, Eliza, Sarah [Sayer], Gray, Jr., and Waller, and moved to Blount County, Tennessee. They made the journey with their household possessions in covered wagons drawn by oxen.
>
> The family settled near Montvale, at the foot of Chilhowee Mountain,[2] a community to become famous as Montvale Springs, a favorite nineteenth-century watering spa. There Smith owned a farm and grist mill. He apparently was a man of many interests. He surveyed Chilhowee Mountain, had business concerns in Maryville, and publicized East Tennessee's attractions to the prospective British emigrant. He made at least one brief return trip to his native land, for in 1842 he was living at Pentonville, London, where he published this volume and a pamphlet entitled, "A Description of Improved Farms in East Tennessee."
>
> With the exception of that visit, he seems to have lived the remainder of his life as a merchant in Maryville. . . . He died

> on September 2, 1875, and is buried in Magnolia Cemetery, Maryville. His wife's body was brought to Magnolia Cemetery and his daughters Eliza and Sarah also are buried there. His obituary reads in part: "Mr. Smith had an extensive acquaintance, and was respected by all who knew him. Much of his time for many years was devoted to merchandising, and he was noted for the politeness and civility with which he treated his customers, and in fact all with whom he met. He was one of those rare specimens of humanity with whom we seldom meet at the present day, viz; a well read man posted on all subjects upon which it became necessary for him to talk."
>
> Smith had descendants through his daughter, Eliza (Smith) Henry, and his son, Gray Smith, Jr., who are still living in Blount County and elsewhere. His great-granddaughter, Gray Webb (Mrs. David W. [Proffitt]), of Maryville, has in her possession portraits of Smith, of his mother, of his sister, Mary (Smith) Moffat, and of his two daughters. Mrs. [Proffitt] also has Smith's naturalization papers and his passport, the latter signed by Daniel Webster, Secretary of State.[3]

When William Henry died in 1864, Margaret's mother, Eliza, was left a widow with five small children, two girls and three boys. During the difficult years following the war, Eliza's father and sister, Sarah (Sallie to the family) [Sayer] Smith lived with her family. Although the adults struggled with finances, the home was a place of culture where the children were encouraged to read and study. They attended public and private schools in Maryville, and later the two girls and two of the boys entered the Preparatory Department of Maryville College. Margaret and her sister, Sarah (listed as Sallie Mahala in the enrollment ledger), graduated with baccalaureate degrees. Sarah married General Robert N. Hood and lived in Knoxville; Margaret was a teacher and in 1903 became the scholarship secretary at Maryville College; William Jasper Henry, Jr., was a contractor and builder in Maryville; Gray Smith Henry moved to Oakland, California; and John Smith Henry worked for Southern Railway, whose headquarters were in Bristol, Tennessee.

For four years, Eliza managed the college boarding hall, to secure an education for her children. Board cost each student $2 a week. Eliza purchased the food and prepared three meals a day, seven days a week. The dining room and kitchen for the boarding hall were located in the basement of Baldwin Hall. Other kitchens were available, at a small cost to students, in Baldwin four kitchens and Memorial Hall ten kitchens for those who preferred to board themselves.

Religious observance was central to college life in the nineteenth century. Because of the lack of space on the campus, most services and meetings were held at New Providence Presbyterian Church during the antebellum years. But by the 1870s, the chapel in Anderson Hall provided adequate facilities for such events. In 1877, the college held the first annual revival series that later came to be known as the February Meetings. The leader was Dr. Nathan Bachman, who had been a member of the Maryville College Board of Directors and the pastor of Second Presbyterian Church in Knoxville before turning to general evangelistic work in 1876. During this first series of meetings, Sam Wilson and Margaret Henry, along with a group of close friends, committed their lives to Christ. A few days after her conversion, Margaret joined New Providence Presbyterian Church, where she served in many capacities for the remainder of her life.

The revival series ignited an interest in foreign missions on the campus. Margaret caught the missionary spirit and dedicated herself to foreign service. As she prepared spiritually, mentally, and financially for this work, Margaret taught school for four years at Miller's Cove in Blount County, near Shannondale in Knox County, in Lexington, Mississippi, and in Rockford in Blount County.

In 1882, five former Maryville College students went abroad as foreign missionaries of the Presbyterian Church: Francina Porter (Japan), Margaret Henry (Japan), Cora Bartlett (Persia), Rev. James Rogers (Persia), and Rev. Samuel Wilson (Mexico). On the voyage to Japan,

Margaret fell during a severe storm and sustained a serious spinal injury. The injury did not improve, and Margaret, much to her sorrow, had to return home a year later. For many months she was unable to work. Finally, she began teaching again, first in Maryville and then for one year in the Knoxville city schools. She moved back home in 1890 and accepted a position as matron of Baldwin Hall at Maryville College. In addition to her duties as matron, Margaret served for a short time as an instructor in English and German until a full-time professor was appointed. Then, in 1895 and from that time forward, Margaret served as an instructor in the English branches of the Preparatory Department. She was a conscientious and thorough teacher who took a deep, personal interest in each of her students.

In the late 1890s, Margaret joined the Chilhowee Club and the Tuesday Club, federated women's clubs in Maryville. The members of both organizations were looking for ways to serve the community and decided to commit their time and resources to educational work in the mountains of East Tennessee. In the fall of 1901, Margaret proposed an idea to the clubs: to hold a short-term summer school in a mountain valley during July and August, use state textbooks, teach music, hold Sabbath-school and preaching services, and provide a teacher. The first summer school opened in Walker Valley the next summer.

While Margaret was busily engaged teaching in the Preparatory Department and providing leadership for the educational work in the mountains, two colleagues were following her endeavors with interest: Rev. Elmer Waller, professor of mathematics and secretary of the faculty, and Dr. Samuel Tyndale Wilson, president. As leaders of the college, both men knew of the great need for scholarships and money to fund student help. Dr. Wilson, at the suggestion of Rev. Waller, asked Margaret if she would be willing to travel in the North to raise funds to secure an education for future students at Maryville College. Understandably, Margaret struggled with the decision, doubting her ability to be successful. Finally, a year later, she agreed to become the scholarship secretary.

Rev. Elmer Waller

From the beginning, however, she was successful and found many people interested in the children of the Southern Appalachians. Her itineraries were strenuous. At least twice during her thirteen-year tenure, she was "on the wing" (traveling) for the entire school year. Other years, she was gone for six or more months. Generally, she spoke once each day and two times on Sunday. Often, each event during the week was held in a different city. Her audiences were Daughters of the American Revolution chapters; various organizations for men, women, and children; churches; schools; and individuals. When she returned to her home base each evening, Margaret spent several hours writing letters.

At each meeting, Margaret hoped to receive a $50 scholarship, which provided one student a room and tuition for a year. Yet Margaret's work was greater than a single scholarship. She raised funds for the college hospital and for the personal needs of individual students. She wrote thousands of letters to donors who gave small and large gifts, to students who needed encouragement, and to friends throughout the Northeast.

When at home, she taught a Sunday school class, visited the homes of students in remote mountain valleys, taught a class in the Preparatory Department, and checked thank-you notes written by students before they were mailed.

When Margaret began her thirteenth year as scholarship secretary in 1915, she left Maryville in October, prepared to stay in the Northeast until June. That fall, she spent several weeks in Philadelphia, Pennsylvania, meeting with groups and individuals throughout the state. Then she headed to New York and made her headquarters at the Hotel Rutledge for Women, a twelve-story building on the corner of Lexington Avenue and Thirtieth Street. From there she took trains to New Jersey, Connecticut, Massachusetts, and various cities in New York state for the many speaking engagements she had booked for the year. During the Christmas holiday, Margaret went to West Conshohocken, Pennsylvania, to visit a former student, Dr. Elizabeth Winter. She was the daughter of Preston and Matilda Winter of Maryville and the director and physician in charge of the Inwood Sanitarium, which opened in 1898.

Margaret arrived in Maryville from her long year in the North on Saturday, June 10. She taught her Philathea class (for young women of the church) on Sunday for the first time since October. Two days later, despite being ill, she visited her sister, Sarah Mahala Henry Hood, who was doing mountain settlement work in a small community near the Chilhowee Mountain. Sarah had succeeded Margaret as chairman of the settlement work for the Tennessee State Federation of Women's Clubs. The next day, Margaret consulted a physician, who ordered her to bed. Reluctantly, she followed the doctor's orders but requested that a stenographer be sent to her home. For ten days, she dictated letters and planned her itinerary for the fall. As her condition became worse, she entered a hospital in Knoxville. On July 6, an operation was performed and on Friday morning, July 7, she passed away without regaining consciousness. Many of the letters that she dictated had not yet reached their destinations. But the fall itinerary, left on the table by her bed, was ready for the next scholarship representative from Maryville College.

Dr. Samuel Tyndale Wilson

Dr. Samuel Tyndale Wilson, Margaret's college classmate, gave the address at her funeral on July 9, 1916, at New Providence Presbyterian Church. He assessed her outstanding work as scholarship secretary this way:

> Her marvelous success was due probably to four elements of strength: (1) To her genuine and transparent sincerity and tense earnestness. (2) To her unceasing prayerfulness and her absolute faith in God's leadership in even the details of her campaigns. (3) To her natural and heart-winning eloquence. . . . (4) To her remarkable social qualities. Every day she was the guest of some home, and so engaging and winning was her personality that her hosts became her warm and enduring friends, and for her they exerted their influence even year after year. . . .
>
> When we attempt to appraise the great work she had done even as Scholarship Secretary, leaving out of account all the other

> conspicuous and far-reaching service rendered as one of the best of teachers and as one of the most active of philanthropic and church workers—a service in itself enough to make us pronounce her one of the very useful women of the generation—we feel entirely unable to make a proper appraisement of that work.[4]

In her thirteen years as scholarship secretary, Margaret raised a grand total of $122,692.91. Approximately 84 percent of the total went to current scholarships and self-help. Other contributions went to the hospital endowment fund, toward the salary for a nurse, for hospital and other equipment, and to the agricultural department. As early as 1906, Margaret was telling donors about the need for permanent scholarships to secure the education of future students. More than $13,000 from the grand total established the Endowed Scholarship Program, now the Maryville Fund.

For months and years after her death, Margaret's many friends contributed, through a memorial fund, to the Margaret E. Henry Endowed Scholarship, which had been established on May 12, 1906, by friends from the North. As late as 1944, a contribution came from a church in Philadelphia, Pennsylvania. And today, one hundred years later, Margaret's great work continues through the life of a current student at Maryville College who has received the Margaret E. Henry Endowed Scholarship.

Home address.

Address until about May 20, 1909,
541 Lexington Ave., New York,
March 10th, 1909.

Mrs. R. N. Gere,
336 W. Onondaga St.,
Syracuse, N. Y.

My dear Mrs. Gere:

Now that I have come back to New York from my long itinerary of nearly three weeks, I must take time to thank you for the kindly way in which you took me by the hand when I entered your church and welcomed me to the prayer meeting service. I saw your face among the women at the Congregational Church, and I wanted to speak to you, but you had slipped away before I had the chance to do so.

I have asked them to send you some of our college literature from the home office. I have also sent you a little book called "The Southern Mountaineers," written by the president of our College, Rev. S. T. Wilson, D. D.

You must know how intensely interested I am in this work of raising a scholarship fund for the boys and girls of the Southern mountains. I believe that your interest has been so awakened that you will pray for me in my work as I go before strange audiences in this great, busy Northland in the hope of interesting them in my work. Dear Mrs. Gere, this is not an easy thing to do. If I stopped for a moment to think of myself I should be stage-struck before so many audiences. Always the young people of the Southern mountains come to my rescue, and when I see them as in a vision, and think of their needs, I forget all else save them, and then it is easy to give my message.

Thanking you for your kindly words of cheer and for your interest in my work, I am

Sincerely and gratefully yours,

Margaret's Love of Her Work

My whole heart is in this work, and well it may be, for I belong to this mountain people on the paternal side and was born at the foot of Chilhowee Mountain here in East Tennessee.

—Margaret E. Henry

CHAPTER TWO

The Deep-Valley Folk of the Southern Mountains

Margaret Henry's heart was always in the mountains. From the first moment she felt the cold water of Little River to her last view of the misty, blue mountains from her sleeping porch in Maryville, Margaret was a part of the Southern Mountains and the people who lived there. As scholarship secretary, she traveled in the Northeast for months at a time raising money for student scholarships. Although Margaret was dedicated to Maryville College and its students, she was always eager to return home.

As she wrote in a letter,

> My peaceful valley of East Tennessee seems lovelier to me than ever now that I feel myself more of a fixture here. . . . [She had traveled for nine months during 1913–14.] The blue mountains on either side seem higher and call me with a voice, almost irresistible, to plunge into their leafy depths, scale their frowning heights, or linger in their shadowy valleys.[1]

In August 1912, Margaret scaled the "frowning heights" of Thunderhead, the highest peak on the western end of the Southern Mountains. She traveled fifteen miles by train to the Riverside Station, where she was met by her cousin, John Dunn, as she recounted:

From there it was a jolting drive with him across Dry Valley to the foot of Scott Mountain, where my cousins, the Dunns live. It is well worth a trip into the heart of the mountains just to meet this big, hearty, wholesome, healthful, happy family. Sixteen children and three grandchildren have been raised beneath this hospitable rooftree by my cousins, Will and Dolly Dunn. The life here seems almost patriarchal to one who is a guest, sitting on the porch of the old home. The smoke comes curling up from the smaller homes of the children who have married and settled nearby. The old barn, with its fields about it, showed us some of the finest stock in the country, while seven cows stood patiently night and morn in contented rows, to be milked, the saucy calves of some of them enlivening the scene as they came butting in for their share. The orchards, stretching far up on the mountainside, though not overladen with fruit this year, yet served us an abundance of apples and peaches from the horn of plenty. At night, a fat feather bed and a fatter feather pillow lulled me to pleasant dreams. Six enlarged photographs, almost life size, stared at me from the ceiled walls of the parlor where I slept. Some of these spoke of days gone by when these hands of toil cleared the rocky mountain slopes and paved the way for this younger generation to enter into a richer heritage. In the dining room a homemade sideboard told of the loving efforts of my cousin John to gladden his mother's heart with something modern and up-to-date, while the kitchen had two new corner cupboards, fresh from his hand, and doors and windows had been screened.

At the gray dawn we were all astir. . . . There was a hurried breakfast before sunup for ourselves; then the provisions for the journey were done up in sacks and packed behind the saddles of our horses. I was privileged to ride Prince, well named, for he is a prince among horses, although a kicker at time in harness and given to rolling over on his side in still waters, irrespective of the rider on his back. Prince bore me up, up, up, by many a winding way through dark avenues of rhododendrons, up Laurel Creek for two miles, through the rocky creek bed, the stream murmuring in cascades, rushing past us in tiny silver waterfalls, through which we climbed in spite of slippery rocks and dashing sprays.

Soon we came to a welcome stretch of meadow in a little dell among the mountains, with a tangle of rank meadow grass on either side. On we went, past a deserted cabin, where the fruit trees of a long neglected orchard, bending with fruit, told of thrift in days gone by. Then we came to a newly made road leading into the depths of the forest and straight to the little log cabin of a woman from the outer world, who has taken up a timber tract and must live upon it in order to hold it. We wondered much about "the lady of the solitude," whether she is old or young, plain or beautiful, married or unmarried; whether even now bright flowers are blossoming in that lonely yard, and whether household pets or household comrades lighten the loneliness of her lot.

Up again, we came to the heights, where one could look down upon the newly built cabin of an old man who lives all alone in the solitude of the Big [Smoky Mountains], alone save for his friends, the wild wood creatures and the droning music of his bees, whose delicious honey, gathered from the wild and woodsy sweets of the mountains, has made the old man famous for miles around.

Soon, we came to the musical waters of the West Prong of Little River and mourned the bare mountain slopes on either side, left so by the lumber company that has for some years had in tow the laying low of these forest giants in the heart of which treasures of silver and gold lie hidden until converted into the coin of the realm in the great marts of the outer world. We passed miles of mountain territory devastated by the terrible forest fires that had swept everything before them, leaving only charred stumps and a mournful wreckage of majestic forests, while a feeble growth of shrubs and vines in tender compassion sought to cover all this desolation with the soft tendrils of green.

On we went again till the air grew thin, on and on to the Cold Spring, two miles from the summit. Here we stopped for dinner and made fried chicken and all other edibles fly. . . . For our guest we had the owner of a little valley, who was out on the mountain looking after his stock. . . . This little valley has neither school nor church, since only two or three families live there, and it is only as these climb out of the solitude of those deep depths that they get a breath of the learning and religion of the outer world.

At the Cold [Spring] we sent our horses back and prepared for the last steep climb, carrying, strapped on our backs, all the baggage that the horses had brought thus far. The four of us moved, one behind the other on the mountain trail, and it is needless to say that I brought up the rear, bearing on my back some of the necessities and comforts of civilization, few of which I could use for lack of privacy in the herders' cabin. . . .

It is very like the swift changing moods of the mountains that the minute the sound of our horses' hoofs melted into silence down the mountain slopes, out of a clear sky gathered hastily but most bountifully from the mist and dew and fog a heavy rain began to pour down upon us. It filled the brim of my mountain hat and flowed in torrents thence down my back. It slouched through the open work of my heavy sandals; it dripped from my mohair skirt; it blinded my eyes; . . . it fell upon our tin cans like rain upon a roof; it threatened to waterlog the savory edibles of our temporary larder and to convert the meal into hasty pudding on the spot. . . . But against all this . . . the dauntless courage of our spirits bore us ever up and on to the point where we cross the state-line from Tennessee into North Carolina, nearly 6000 feet above the sea level.

How good it seemed to set our feet at last on the velvety bluegrass of the mountain top and look eagerly for the blue smoke of Spence's Cabin, where the herders live and shelter all who come their way, be they many or few. How like music after our weary climb seemed the tinkle of mountain bells on pigs, sheep and cattle alike. . . . The little cabin had two rooms and a loft, an open fire, a long table, two long backless slab benches, several sheepskins, one wash pan, one comb, one towel, one cake of soap doing service for all the others though we had our own. Here we slept for two nights in a rough slab bed, eight men over us in the loft, four on the same floor with us, minus undressing, minus pillows, minus sheets, but not minus sleep. . . . Our herder hosts gave us right of way in the cabin, and surely, we were a motley crowd gathered there. Let me see—there was a moonshiner looking after his still on Eagle Creek; a refugee from the law, with a relative to keep him in tow; a herder from the cove below, and his shy little lad who never took off his old slouch wool hat, though he smiled at me from under its brim, a smile like the breaking of sunshine through a mountain fog. There was a father and son from a distant valley, come to look after their flock of sheep; four assistant herdsmen, and our party of four. . . .

First and last while there, we listened to many tales of wintry winds, of snowbound men and cattle in untimely April or May snowstorms; tales of men lost and buried under winter snows, who were found in the spring with the money of their last earthly payday clenched in their hands. . . . There were talks of the hunting dogs that had trailed after game, past all human habitation and had never returned to tell in mute dog fashion of prowess or brave adventure. . . . There were tales of men caught in bear traps [and] of men who had been scorched and seared in the terrible forest fires of the mountains. There were tales . . . of [newfangled] school systems that had consolidated the public schools of a few valleys "leaving some little chaps to git thar, and some stranded too high and dry and fur off to get thar." We were told that a stone could be rolled from where we sat to the door of a still that no revenue officer would ever be able to find. There were stirring talks of bear hunts, of rattlesnake dens . . . of the lonesomeness when the cattle all go winding down the mountain slopes in September and their deep tones of silvery bells no longer waken the mountain echoes. There were talks of the wonderful instinct of the cattle in leaving the mountain tops and seeking shelter below when a storm is brooding the heavens.

The second day we spent in climbing all the high peaks near and far, Rocky Point [now called Rocky Top], Thunderhead Peak, and Little Bald. In that pure air we climbed all these lengthening miles without weariness, though we made bold inroads upon the rapidly diminishing contents of our larder—but what mattered it? Every night the lucky fishermen brought us fifty speckled trout for supper, and the hunters added squirrels fresh from the forest trees. . . . It was a day never to be forgotten, for, from the Thunderhead we could look down into Riverside, Tuckaleechee, Cades Cove, and Wears Valley, and see them lying like so many emerald isles in the midst of a sea of glory. The faint outline of the Cumberlands was visible across the great valley of East Tennessee, and on clear nights the lights of Maryville and Knoxville can be seen. . . .

But it was the trip to Little Bald that took fast hold of my [heartstrings], and it is here that I feel that I must pitch a tent all other summers of my life. The summit of Little Bald is one glorious velvety slope of bluegrass. . . . Lying prone on the mountainside, with eyes half closed, one can see all shades of color in clouds and shadows, in purple and saffron, in emerald and sapphire, opal and amethyst. . . . How I shall dream of this vision of beauty when the great centers of influence close about me this winter, where the sky is only a leaden patch over my head, where the heights are all of man's building, where the "rattlers" are the strident notes of traffic, and the cattle bells are the silvery chimes from cathedral towers; where the winding trails are found in faint semblance in the city parks; where the wild wood notes and the [backwoods] characters are cheaply imitated in the movies; where the masterpieces for Nature are only faintly reproduced in the great art galleries of our nation; where the trammels of civilization, the strict adherence to the amenities and courtesies of life set one to longing for the rough homespun characters of the mountains, the good hard [common sense] of her people, with their ability to put truth in a nutshell, to sift the wheat from the chaff in the polished guests from the outer world, for their unselfish kindliness of heart, their absolute sincerity, for their hatred of falsehood and deception and, no matter how sinful they themselves may be, their perfect scorn of those who have drifted from their moorings and lost their faith in God. . . . Now that I am home again, how often, from my sleeping porch, I look away to the heights of Old Smoky, Thunderhead and the Bald, twenty-five miles away. . . . From this time forth there is a bond between us, we have spoken heart to heart.[2]

Margaret was drawn to children like the "shy little lad" in the slouch wool hat. Her letters are filled with stories about the mountain settlement work started by the Tennessee State Federation of Women's Clubs in 1901. Margaret, a club member, was named chairman of the new program. After she began traveling for Maryville College, she continued to help with the summer schools that had been established in several remote valleys. Many of her college students worked with her. Margaret told a friend, "The children of the mountains are so serious, indeed, we have to teach them games and laughter and motion songs."[3] The first summer school was held in Walker Valley, and Margaret remembered "one little girl, . . . who, when she saw the first flag waving in the breeze of her mountain valley, said, 'How did the children git that thar red rag on the top of that thar pole?' To her, the Stars and Stripes was no more than a red rag, yet her ancestors had been among those who struck and took blows for liberty in the dark days of the Revolution."[4]

In 1901, access to Walker Valley was simply a log placed across the swift water of Little River. Few supplies could be carried across the log and over the three miles on a very rough trail to the school. Visits to the valley folk in the winter or at Christmas were impossible. By 1909, a bridge had been built, and Margaret visited the valley frequently when she was at home. In a letter to Mrs. Carl Viets of Connecticut, she shared a vivid description of the children:

> The children of Walker Valley never had a toy in all their lives until our summer school work was carried into the Valley. The girls had never seen a doll. The boys did not know how to play with a top or with marbles. One boy who was given a knife and a hollow rubber ball at the same time, took his knife and cut the ball open to see what was inside, and when nobody could put it together again for him he cried as if his heart would break.
>
> The first time I took a box of doughnuts into the Valley, the children were so delighted with them, they could not bear to eat them. They spent the best part of the afternoon in looking through the holes, while I sat in the background trying hard to keep my face straight. The next year I took some animal crackers. There were some tears shed as an elephant lost its trunk, or a cow its horns.
>
> I would not have you think that these children are altogether sad without toys. I sometimes think that the children in cities, who have a nursery full of toys, grow weary of them and want still more, are less happy than the little children of the mountains who can take a pebble, a shell, a pine cone, or a smooth stick, and with these devise games enough to keep them happy the live long day.[5]

During her travels in the Northeast to raise money for scholarships, Margaret made many lifelong friendships. Frequently these friends sent

Walker Valley

boxes of clothes, books, and small gifts to Margaret for the children and the mountain schools. Her letters are filled with descriptions of the children who were delighted with the "embarrassment of riches," of young men and women looking for the strength to leave the mountains to seek an education, and of adults who were sometimes struggling with the changes coming to their mountain communities. The following vignettes reveal much about life in the Southern Mountains.

Pennies Given to Mountain Children

On one of many visits to Walker Valley, Margaret gave a few pennies to the children of Moll Stinnett, who lived in a small, one-room cabin perched on the side of the mountain. Margaret paints this word picture in a letter written in January 1914 to Mrs. H. G. MacDonald of Wilkinsburg, Pennsylvania: "I imagine they will walk from their valley all the way to Townsend, 6 or 7 miles, in order to spend their pennies at the mountain store. I should like to know their choice of purchases, and I know how they will be clutched tightly in sturdy mountain hands and spread out on the floor to be gazed at until the novelty wears off."[6]

Christmas Candy

Donors from the North sent Christmas gifts for the children living in remote mountain valleys. When possible, Margaret suggested appropriate gifts of clothing, games, books, and sweet treats. In November 1913, she wrote to Anne Waite, secretary of the Cheerful Workers Circle of the King's Daughters of the Greenwich Presbyterian Church in New York to explain the children's preference for stick candy: "In selecting candy for the children, please do not buy chocolate candy, as the children of the mountains never having had it, do not like it. They prefer the red stick candy, and this, of course, is much cheaper and will go farther."[7]

Grace Buchanan, a Prospective Eighth-Grade Student

Margaret described the home of Grace Buchanan to Bertha Douglas of Aspinwall, Pennsylvania, a prospective donor, in a letter written in November 1914: "Grace's home is literally on the bleak [mountainside] above Happy Valley. It is one of the loneliest places, since it is so off the beaten track that they never see any one passing by, unless it be a hunter, a revenue officer, or a moonshiner."[8]

A Mountain Boy from Dry Valley

In a letter of thanks to Harriette Campfield for a $50 scholarship given to Earl McCampbell, Margaret described both Earl's appearance and his childhood on a small farm in Townsend. She wanted Earl's benefactor to know his background and to visualize him as a student on the Maryville College campus.

> He is a tall, shy lad, with gray eyes and light brown hair. His mother is one of those earnest, faithful mothers of the

> mountains who is willing to make a great sacrifice to spare Earl from home. His father is a [hardworking] mountaineer, who had no education himself and perhaps very little ambition for his children. . . . They have really laid too heavy burdens on Earl, and I wondered that he could grow under the heavy strain of farm work that has been his since he was five years old. He ploughed when he was six years old and could dig a straight furrow across a mountain field. There is no danger that Earl will not do his part in the way of work. He is also doing splendid classroom work.[9]

An Older Student

Cora Hopkins was twenty years old when she enrolled in the lowest level of the Preparatory Department on September 7, 1909. Her mother had died when Cora was two and her father seven years later. She moved in with an older brother and his family, but at age thirteen, she dropped out of school to work full-time in a box factory to help with expenses. Nevertheless, during these difficult years, she never lost her desire for an education.

The Good Cheer Club of East Orange, New Jersey, provided scholarships for Cora for several years. Margaret kept the club members informed about Cora's progress:

> Cora was not a young girl when she entered college, and I hardly dared hope that she would be able to do more than graduate from the preparatory department, which has a four year course. She has a burning desire to complete this course and enter the college department, which is four years longer. The more I have to do with students through my work here, the more I appreciate the grit and perseverance in them and an ideal that makes them hold on until they realize their hopes and dreams.
>
> We have never had a girl who made more rapid progress than has Cora. She always keeps ahead of the required number of credits. . . . She is a girl of rare good [common sense]; she

> knows how to do a great many things well, and has the tact to get along with others.
>
> Cora has never had a vacation since she came to college, as she takes summer work as soon as college closes. Her first vacation she spent as a helper in a home. For two summers now, she has been one of the workers in a settlement school in Happy Valley. She has been such a conscientious worker, and has endeared herself to the people of this beautiful valley. . . .
>
> Many times you have made Cora's heart glad by the kindnesses which you have shown her, not only in keeping up her scholarship, but in the Christmas boxes, which she has thoroughly enjoyed and shared with others.[10]

Cora graduated from Maryville College in the class of 1917 with a major in science. In the fall following graduation, she became the principal of a school in Kentucky.

Marbles

Occasionally, gifts came from children. In January 1914, Margaret wrote a letter of thanks to Paul Black of Wilkinsburg, Pennsylvania, for a box of marbles, which was given to two brothers, Hobson and Joe Stinnett: "Thank you very much for the box of marbles which you sent to your 'Dear New Friend in the Mountains.' Hobson is about eleven years old, and Joe is younger but I think that it would break his heart to have Hobson receive all the marbles."[11]

A Drowning

On June 3, 1910, Margaret was in New York preparing to return home after many months in the Northeast. As she was writing the last of several thank-you notes, she received a letter from a mother in Walker Valley. Margaret included this message from the valley in the letter of thanks to Mr. and Mrs. Walter S. Lewis, members of St. Paul Presbyterian Church in Philadelphia, Pennsylvania:

> Susie, 3 years old . . . was drowned in the swift river just in front of their little log cabin. Annie, an older sister, eight years old, sprang into the deep, swirling waters to save Susie, but could not do it and almost lost her own life in the attempt. When little Susie was buried in that lonely valley, the Settlement School was closed for the time and there was no one to say a word or offer a prayer when she was lowered into the small grave on the mountainside.[12]

Butter-and-Egg Mother

Margaret shared the following story with Mrs. Robert H. Cushman of Monson, Massachusetts, and her Sunday school class of boys in a thank-you letter written in January 1912 for a gift to the scholarship fund:

> Last summer, at about half past six every morning, I used to see a mother and her two sons passing our home. The mother always carried a basket of butter and eggs, and her sons drew a small wagon of early vegetables. I began to take vegetables of her, and became deeply interested not only in the sweet-faced mother, but also in the two boys who were helping her to run the little farm on the edge of the town.
>
> One day the mother opened up her heart to me and told me that her husband had been marshal in one of the mountain towns of East Tennessee. He was shot down while bravely doing his duty in executing the law. The loss and sorrow filled the mother's heart with a great desire to educate her sons, so she moved to Maryville, bought this little farm and is bravely struggling to pay for it. She was so happy when I told her that she could send Henry to college and that I would raise a scholarship for him during the year.[13]

Gifts for Sallie Ann

The Thursday Morning Fort Nightly Club of Dorchester, Massachusetts, gave a $50 scholarship for Sallie Ann Stinnett of Walker Valley in 1912. As the Christmas season approached, Margaret wrote to club president, Mrs. Lewis Tracy, to suggest Christmas gifts for Sallie Ann: "handkerchiefs, stockings #9, warm gloves #6, hair ribbons or neckware."[14]

A Gift of Soap

In December 1910, Margaret received a gift of Fels-Naptha soap from the Princeton Presbyterian Church of Philadelphia, Pennsylvania. In a letter of thanks, she wrote,

> Yours is one of the most practical gifts that I have received, and if you knew how many homes in the mountains stood in need of soap you would rejoice that you had sent it. One mother in one of the little log cabins told me once, when I was visiting her, that she had been powerful saving of the soap I had given her the summer before. She had laid it up on the logs so she would have enough left to wash the children all round by the time I got back to her. The soap that has gone back into the mountains has created a sentiment in favor of soap. They put forth an effort to get it, though the poverty is often so great that the hunger for bread must come first.[15]

A Visit to Hattie's Home

In August 1907, Mrs. Percy Wightman of University Heights, New York, sent $50 for a second scholarship. In a letter of thanks written in September 1907, Margaret described her most recent visit to the home of Hattie Kirkland, the recipient of this generous gift:

> I spent a very happy day. . . . There are nine children in the family and I gave them a penny apiece, which caused more excitement in that plain little mountain home than if I had given a hundred dollars to a like number of children in some beautiful

New York home. As I sat at the table on the little back porch and ate dinner from a poor, washed-out red tablecloth, but surrounded by the group of rosy-cheeked children, my mind went wandering back to that dainty luncheon in your home and I rejoiced that through that luncheon hour with you, the influence was wrought that would change conditions in this little Greenbrier Valley.

Mr. Kirkland is one of the strongest characters in the Valley. It is a most lawless valley, and he is the only one who has the moral courage to report people and make them suffer the penalty of the law for nightly marauding and secret distilling of whisky and drunken brawls at the logging camp. They are all afraid of him, and this fear is wholesome though I have feared at times for his life.

Hattie is a very bright girl. She brought her sister to call on me when I was in the Valley, and I could notice such a difference in her ease and also in her conversational powers. . . . I used to enjoy seeing her going after the cows, a merry barefoot girl wading up the clear mountain stream, bending under the rhododendrons, climbing around boulders of rock, jumping like a squirrel across fallen trees on the rough trail up the mountains for the cows. She brought them home to the music of the [cowbells]. As I watched her, I thought of the days when she will begin wandering in other pastures and come bringing home all the wonderful possibilities of life as college unfolds them to her.[16]

Pen-Pal Inquiry

In 1912 the students at Bradford Academy in Bradford, Massachusetts, provided a $50 scholarship for Mary Clark, a fourth-year student in the Preparatory Department. As the year passed, the students at Bradford became interested in the young people from the mountains of East Tennessee. One young woman wrote to Margaret asking for the name of a girl from the mountains with whom she could correspond. Margaret replied promptly: "Each scholarship girl here in college is already assigned to some individual donor or organization and must confine her correspondence to those granting scholarship help."

With regard to the young people living in the mountains, Margaret explained,

> It is hard for you to understand the conditions in the remote mountain valleys—you do not know how a poor little mountain girl would tremble and hesitate to open correspondence with a cultured girl of an Eastern Academy. Her awakening must come through the workers sent to the valley, rather than from those who have never been in touch with the mountain life.[17]

Married at Sixteen

Margaret often spoke during morning worship services at churches in the northeast. Class 31 of Memorial Presbyterian Church in Rochester, New York, heard Margaret's message and sent a $50 scholarship. In a letter written in November 1912, to Susan Howell, a member of Class 31, Margaret expressed thanks and shared information about the scholarship student:

> I have assigned for your special student a young girl from North Carolina, by the name of Dora Dennis. An earnest physician and his wife, who had gone to North Carolina for special surgical work among the men who were building a railroad through the mountains, became interested in Dora and influenced her to come to Maryville.[18]

On January 13, 1913, Margaret updated the class on Dora's progress:

> Your student Dora Dennis is still with us, and shows great improvement since she entered in the fall. Her shyness has worn off, and her expression has grown very sweet and winning. . . . Just before Christmas she told her teacher she had written an "original story," and when she gave it to her to read, it was found to be so very original, that I made a copy of it, thinking you would be interested.[19]

A year after Dora enrolled at Maryville, Margaret wrote this sad letter in September 1913:

> After all that you and Class 31 did for Dora Dennis last year, it grieves me more than I can tell you to have to write you the sorrowful news that she is married and that, at the age of sixteen. She married a young neighbor boy of the mountains who is only a year or two older than herself.
>
> My first thought was that her year in college was utterly thrown away, but we must not think that. We cannot tell how far-reaching its influence may be, and if Dora has children of her own, no doubt she will have higher ideals in educating them.
>
> You would have to understand the mountain conditions to know how soon the young people in the mountains develop and how prone they are to give up childhood and girlhood and marry at the age of thirteen, fourteen, fifteen and sixteen. A girl is considered an old maid at eighteen.
>
> Our church schools have done all in their power to counteract this evil, but it will not be overcome in one generation, and pretty, bright, sturdy, joyous Dora Dennis is another child sacrificed to the ignorance of the mountains.
>
> She has the lovely quilt you sent her last spring, and I cannot but believe that the long list of loyal friends whose names are inscribed thereon will be like so many voices calling to her to do her best to undo the mistake of her youth by making the very most of her life in her narrow surroundings.[20]

A Mountain Father and Mother

Eleanor G. Parks of East Allegheny, Pennsylvania, provided a scholarship for seventeen-year-old Fred Whitehead from Happy Valley for the 1912–13 school year. Margaret described Fred's parents and his desire for an education in a letter to Miss Parks written in October 1912:

> Fred's father and mother are plain, hard-working, industrious people. They have a poor little farm, although I am glad to say that the father has given a great deal of attention to fruit culture. As the railroad is not within six miles of Happy Valley, I am hoping that he can find a better market for it.
>
> The father is a most interesting man. Although uneducated, he has a keen mind and much native wit. He is a thinker and very fond of argumentation, especially along religious lines. He never argues for the sake of being convinced himself, but would always bring his opponent to his way of thinking, if that were possible. He had hoped that Fred would be satisfied with the public schools of his own valley, but Fred could not be satisfied with this foretaste of better things and the appeal was made to us to open the way for him to come to college.
>
> The mother is a sturdy, motherly woman, who has a goodly household of children, and she rules them with love in an easy-going fashion. She never enters into argument with her husband and his guests, but listens with great admiration as her husband expatiates at great length upon themes too deep for her. She believes that there is more in living religion than in arguing it.[21]

Death of a Student

In September 1910, Margaret wrote a difficult and sad letter to H. Frank Pierson of Orange, New Jersey.

> I am very sorry to write you that your scholarship student, William Alonzo Clark, died the latter part of August in the hospital in Knoxville. His mother was with him during his last days, and some of our college professors also went to see him. Almost to the very last, he thought that God would spare him to carry out his life's plans, although he faced either life or death without fear and with a brave heart.

His mother was a plain, hard-working, uneducated woman, who has had no opportunity herself but was deeply interested in her son's plans for a college education and training in the seminary.

The young men of the college who knew Mr. Clark well say that he was very gifted in speaking in the literary society and that he was never afraid to take a firm stand for the right in the face of any opposition. Last year he used his influence to get a great many of our boys to give up the use of tobacco, and his life as a Christian among his classmates will be felt for many a day.[22]

Differences between Town People and the Mountaineers

Margaret's cousin Lily Henry from Cosby first enrolled at Maryville College in 1904. When Margaret was at home from her travels in the Northeast, Lily was a frequent visitor. In a letter to Mrs. A. Romeya Pierson of Glen Ridge, New Jersey, Margaret wrote about her cousin:

I had a long talk the other evening with my cousin Lily, and she was trying to sum up the differences between the people of the towns and those of the mountains. She has been in college several years and she has been thinking a good deal about it. I think that she has been able to draw very just and accurate conclusions with reference to it. She said, "Cousin Margaret, in the towns"—and she meant Maryville and Maryville College, for she does not know any larger place—"people are more polite than in the mountains. They are so polite that they often say things they do not mean for the sake of pleasing, but in the mountains we say just what we think and people always know where to find us." She also said, that in the towns people helped their neighbors and those who were as well dressed and in the same circumstances when great illness and sorrow was in the home, but in the mountains everybody was willing to help

> everyone else and there was never a night so dark or a road so dangerous that one would not rise up at midnight to go out to a neighbor's and remain as long as there was sorrow or sickness, or suffering.[23]

Nancy Dropped Out

When Nancy Phillips did not return for the new semester, Margaret conveyed her disappointment in a letter to Mrs. J. R. Woodhull, the scholarship donor:

> Many times since college has opened, I have longed to write you, but I have been hoping against hope that Nancy Elizabeth Phillips [a second-year preparatory student from Oneida] would return to us. She came rather late last year, and I felt that she might have to overcome obstacles to get here this year. She has not come, and I take it for granted that her hard, old mother has made it utterly impossible for her to come. . . .
>
> I find with our mountain students that we cannot press our pleas for their return beyond that solid wall of family prejudice and indifference. The door must swing outward when they come to us, but when they can come, it is our joy to do all in our power to satisfy that hunger of heart for better things and for knowledge. It may seem to the Mary Silliman Chapter DAR that this failure of Nancy to return to college is like a failure of her life. I, myself, see her in fancy in the midst of her lonely little mountain valley, with the shadows lying all about her, and that hard, lawless unlovely life of the community beating up against her life with its more refined sensibilities, its unwavering truthfulness, its unswerving sense of right. I know, however, that her days in college will live on in her life and bear fruit. She will never walk a lonely trail of the mountains without hearing the voice that spoke to her while here in college. . . . She will

> never climb those rugged mountain heights but she will feel a keen sense of longing and loss that she was not permitted to climb the far heights of a college education and look out upon a world broader and more beautiful than her narrow valley.[24]

Twilight

Margaret's letters to benefactors were filled with updates about academic progress and work-study jobs. Although these facts and figures were very important to the donors, she frequently took the opportunity to include a short word picture of life in the mountains: "You will be astonished to know that night shuts down early in the mountain valleys because the mountains are so high, and the shadows begin to fall about three o'clock, almost like night during the winter season."[25]

Sending Money Home

Margaret followed the academic progress of her scholarship students and supervised their work-study assignments. When she was on the wing, Molly Caldwell, matron in Baldwin Hall and dean of women, kept Margaret advised about the students.

One such student, Mae Gibson, worked during the summer of 1914 in the college laundry to save money for her incidental expenses. Each month, she sent a portion of her wages home to her family. When Margaret chided her for sending money home instead of saving it for the school year, Mae said, "I can never do too much for my mother after all the hard struggles she has had with poverty to give me a chance to go to college."[26]

Mountain Basket

Throughout her travels in the Northeast, Margaret visited many homes and made many close friends. She often shared a gift from the mountains with them.

In December 1906, Margaret sent a Christmas greeting in the form of a mountain basket to Mrs. M. E. Walling of Victor, New York. She included a description of Christmas in the mountains with the basket.

> It was made in the home of Christopher Columbus Waldrop, whose euphonious nick-name is "Buckeye Cuddy." . . . The holly brightens every lonely ravine of the mountains, so your little basket is filled with the Christmas cheer of the "Southern Highlands." In the little cabin homes, near which it grew, many know nothing of Santa Claus, the giving and receiving of gifts, the Christmas dinner, the reunion of friends, the beautiful spirit of the Christmastide.[27]

Christmas Boxes

During the month of December 1910, Margaret received four large boxes of Christmas gifts from the Princeton Sunday School. Margaret, with the help of friends and members of the College staff, marked each gift with the name of a specific child. In a letter of thanks to the donors, she explained the necessity of marking the gifts and told where the gifts were going:

> In some of the valleys . . . there is no teacher to look after the tree and the marking of the gifts, and since they have so little there might be some rivalry of jealously if the marking was left to any one family. . . .
>
> The doll marked for some little cripple child, I want to give to a dear little boy in the country, who is about three years old. He has no use of his feet or hands, and he has such a bright little face. . . . He will love a doll, for he is often left sitting in the middle of the floor while the family is hard at work outdoors. . . . I have also kept out a ball and a little toy dog for him. . . .
>
> I was so delighted with that box of dolls from the children of the Western Home. It was so dear of them to give each doll a beautiful name. Do thank your young people for such a splendid selection and collection of books. I am glad there were so many

> books for the older children and so many bright picture books for the little children.
>
> Now I must tell you where your boxes are going, now that they have been repacked. The largest one is going to Falls Gap in the heart of the East Tennessee Mountains, away up in the northeastern part of the State, in a beautiful valley where at least a hundred children will be made glad. . . . One little child said to one of our workers some time ago, "Santa Claus never came to our valley until the teachers came here." They have not dared to hope that they could have a Christmas tree this year, and I have not dared to plan for it because of the great number of children. . . .
>
> Another box is to go to Walker Valley. Dora and Lillie Stinnett, two students from that valley, are going home for the Christmas holidays, and they are going to have some of the older boys cut a tree, and they will give out the gifts. . . . There will be plenty of gifts, books, toys, and dolls to gladden the hearts of every one.
>
> Still another box will be sent to Happy Valley. Miss Lena Aikin [a senior in the College Department] who taught there last summer, will take this box and go out to the valley to spend Christmas week and plan for the tree and the carrying out of the Christmas program. She hopes to have recitations, music, a Santa Claus, and everything that she can possibly arrange to make the children happy. She will have a long, cold ride of six miles through the mountains in a lumbering wagon after she leaves the railroad station.[28]

Several smaller packages went to single mothers living in the foothills of the mountains.

Gift of Money

Edna Woodruff, who had visited the college for a brief time, left a gift of money for Margaret, who quickly wrote a letter of thanks:

> I do appreciate the generous impulse of your heart, and now I am writing you to ask if I may keep this amount as a little fund to use when emergency needs arise in the lives of our students. Often a girl receives a message on account of illness or death in the home to return at once, when she may not have a penny with which to make the journey. Again, a poor girl may have to have a new pair of shoes, another may need a gingham dress, while another may lack money for a laboratory fee. I have often wished that some kind friend would grant me a little fund in hand for cases like this, for the scholarship must go directly into the college treasury and stand good for room rent and tuition only.[29]

Two Boxes of Books

The Lamar Memorial Library, a small building located in the center of the campus, contained books that supported the academic curriculum. To encourage the young women to read more, Margaret established a library in Baldwin Hall for classical literature and modern fiction. In October 1912, she wrote a letter of thanks to Sara E. Peirce, president of the Dorchester Daughters of Maine, for a gift of two boxes of books:

> I had the joy of spending a long summer day in unpacking those boxes and bringing forth the treasures, new and old. Please tell the "Bible Lady" that the large Bible was so beautiful and had such splendid print that it has been kept for our Chapel Services. The other Bible has been sent to a country church. . . . It was my joy to have the work of stamping these books with the words "Baldwin Hall Library." Although this library is in Baldwin Hall, seventy girls from Pearsons Hall also will have access to it.
>
> There is a large reading table on the second floor of Baldwin Hall, and I am so anxious to have a few magazines come to us each month, so that our girls may not only have these splendid

> volumes in their library, but in their leisure moments can drop down around this table and find the best current literature at their command. Harpers Magazine and the Ladies Home Journal are already coming to us from friends who are interested in developing in our girls a taste for good reading.[30]

The Gift of a Dollar

As she traveled, Margaret spoke to many organizations with the hope of getting a $50 scholarship for a student. Frequently, individuals attending the meeting gave her a small monetary gift.

In November 1908, Margaret wrote a letter of thanks to Mrs. Edward Croft of Lockport, New York,

> for the dollar which you gave me to use in one of the saddest and most needy homes of the Southern Mountains. I shall apply it to the needs of "Colindy Stinnett" and her children. Her real name should be "Clarinda Stevenson" but these two names, through illiteracy, have become "Colindy Stinnett." Her children are, Elijah, Callie, Hammeralminy, and Freddie Lee. I suppose there must be another baby by this time.
>
> Callie was born in the morning, six years ago. On the afternoon of that same day, the father drove the cow up to the door, and the poor mother had to get up and milk her. . . . I keep this precious dollar separate from all other money and shall write you just how it was invested in behalf of this family. It will go a long way in the mountains toward relieving their needs.[31]

Margaret painted vivid word pictures of the Southern Mountains and the people who lived there when she was on the wing in the Northeast, speaking to women's and men's clubs, DAR chapters, church groups, and schools. In May 1913, she was filled with joy when two friends from Connecticut traveled south for a visit with her and an excursion to the mountains: "We went by log train almost all the way. They exhausted a goodly supply of interjections and adjectives during the first part of the

Maryville College Campus, 1910

journey, but when we reached the deep valleys and lonely trails they were mute with awe, wonder, and admiration."[32]

Margaret had a love of place and a strong sense of family and kinship, characteristics of mountain folk. Yet she lived comfortably and happily in the outside world because of the education her mother, maternal grandfather, and Maryville College had provided. Though she returned frequently to the deep valleys and high peaks to feel the cold water and breathe the crisp air, Margaret dedicated her life to Maryville College and the education of her people.

March 17, 1911.

Mrs. Wm. F. Major,
President of Missionary Society
of First Presbyterian Church,
Ithaca, N. Y.

My dear Mrs. Major:

I am sending you the official report of Josie Crye's standing as a student in Maryville College. "B Plus" means that she has averaged between 85 and 90 in all her work. I think this is a very good record, considering the fact that she had very poor foundation work in her home schools. She has also had to do a good deal of work every day in the dining room of the Co-operative Club to help pay for her board. Coming from a poor home as she does, she has very few clothes, but she does her own laundry work and keeps her dresses always looking well. We have a small loundry connected with the College in which the girls who wish to use it may have this privilege. Joe came to college with one Sunday dress, two gingham dresses, a few shirtwaists and one school skirt. She has kept her clothing in good repair and always looks neat.

Her work has been a little hindered this term on account of serious trouble with her ear. I took her to one of the best specialists of the South, who lives in Knoxville, and he put her under treatment which had to be taken under the supervision and care of her mother. She is getting better and I hope will be back with us at the opening of the Spring Term.

Thanking you for your helpful interest in this bright young girl, and hoping that you will be pleas with her record, I am

Sincerely yours,

Helping a Student

When I started college at the age of 13 in a red calico dress, . . . there were only three buildings on our college campus. I have lived to see many, many changes for the better come to Maryville.

—Margaret E. Henry

CHAPTER THREE

My Dear Old College

In 1870, Anderson Hall, standing high on College Hill, was visible from Main Street in downtown Maryville. When the children of Eliza Henry looked at the new brick edifice from the window of their home, did it appear magnificent to them, or was its size overwhelming? Certainly, there were very few three-story brick buildings in Maryville at that time. Two years later, thirteen-year-old Margaret enrolled at Maryville College and on September 3 walked into a classroom on the third floor of Anderson Hall. Without a doubt, she relived that moment forty years later, when eleven-year-old Sallie Stinnett from Walker Valley declared that "Someday going to Europe would not seem any more wonderful to her than walking from the door of the recitation room."[1]

One hundred thirty-one students were enrolled in 1872 on the sixty-five acre campus. There were three buildings, one academic building and two dormitories, all heated by wood stoves. When Margaret accepted the position of scholarship secretary in 1903, enrollment had grown to 484 students. Acquisition of the College Woods in 1881 had increased the size of the campus to 250 acres. Four academic buildings, two dormitories, a heat plant (1899), and an electric plant (1901) were visible on College Hill. A modern campus was in place, but more work needed to be done. Margaret was ready to join the college forces.

In 1903, she had a desk in the original administrative office, along the front hall of Anderson. Three years later, she and Major Ben Cunningham,

College Hill

treasurer, shared an office and a secretary, Alice Gillingham. By 1910, Margaret needed more space to store records and nonmonetary gifts. More than 650 students were enrolled. Two hundred students had scholarships, and Margaret's correspondence had increased to more than two thousand letters per year. She turned to Dr. Wilson for help: "My work has grown so with the years that it has now reached proportions that to make it altogether successful I need a little college office all my own, free from interruption of any kind and with the entire time of Miss Gillingham given to my work."[2]

Six months later, she and Alice Gillingham moved into the first office on the left down the center hall of Anderson. She described the new office to friends in New Jersey:

> [It is] beautifully equipped with a desk, a filing case, a new typewriter, a typewriter table, a large dictation table, two easy chairs, a waste paper basket, one eighteen-coil radiator, to say nothing of the goodly number of shelves and drawers built in one end of the office. We have christened it "The Jungle," and

> on its walls to the front hang a large copy of Rosa Bonheur's big lion, "Old Nero," and Wm. H. Drake's picture, "On the Lookout," which represents two very great, graceful tigers. There is also a copy of Madame Ronner's cat portrait, mother and kittens. On another wall we have an autumn scene, fashioned especially to remind me of the flight of time and of how soon the winter of age will be upon me. Its companion piece is a portrait of a beautiful child slumbering peacefully upon a downy couch, to remind us that after the work and toil of the day comes rest and oblivion from care. A transparency in the window brings to our imagination the beauty, the rush, and the roar of Niagara's waters. All these pictures I have brought over from home, and they are the gifts of various friends, so that I live in the atmosphere of pleasant memories as I look about me.[3]

When Margaret was on campus, she spent four hours a day teaching in the Preparatory Department and three hours dictating letters. She attended meetings of the Chilhowee Club and often presented programs on Southern literature and mountain social work. She also taught a girls' Bible study class and often took them on picnics in the college woods. "I expect to take my girls to the college grove Saturday for a supper and a good time together. Each one has the privilege of inviting one of the young men of the college. We will have 36 in all. We will have our supper near a lovely spring and running brook, under the shadow of the big forest trees."[4]

Margaret kept in close touch with the campus community when she was on the wing. Dr. Wilson wrote to her regularly, expressing pleasure about contributions to the Forward Fund (campaign to raise $200,000) and giving her information about potential donors:

> I wish you would make the acquaintance of Mr. Albert E. Angier, of the Angier Chemical Company, Allston District, Boston. You know, in the course of three or four years, he has given us a total of $5000 to establish the Angier Self-help Work and Loan Fund. He has been exceedingly kind. . . . I do not

Stream in College Woods

> know very much about him except that he is a liberal, warm-hearted gentleman. I think it would do the cause good if you could get acquainted with him.[5]

Dr. Wilson also wrote of current events on campus: "A new case of small pox developed yesterday. . . . Foolishly he (the student) had not been vaccinated. [There was] a panic at Baldwin last night, over a

Molly Caldwell

supposed man on the third floor. A U.T. man was tied up to a telephone post for two hours on Wednesday night. We have our troubles as well as our victories."[6]

Margaret's sense of humor surfaced when she wrote to Molly Caldwell (Matron in Baldwin Hall) about the man in Baldwin:

> Dr. Wilson wrote me something about a man on the third floor of Baldwin. Is this history or myth? If it is history, I can imagine that you took him by the nape of the neck and flung him halfway over to town. If it was only a ghost—well, in that case, I am not prepared to say what you did. I am sorry that the spring sap is rising in the veins of some of our young people. They always break out in the spring. When we were young, it was different.[7]

On Christmas Day 1911, Margaret and Alice Gillingham were in Buffalo, New York. Margaret later shared the following occurrence in a letter to Dr. Wilson:

> Miss Gillingham and I were called out of bed in the gray dawn of Christmas morning because the building adjoining the YWCA was in flames and had already begun to send its smell of black smoke in the halls. We dressed in a hurry, you may be sure, and were cool enough to get those belongings which pertained to our College work, and unfeminine enough to decide to leave our best Sunday dresses behind if worse came to worst. We were not called upon to make the sacrifice, however, for the firemen fought nobly and mastered the situation before the fire ate its way into the peace and comfort of our Christmas Day.[8]

In 1908, Maryville College needed a hospital. Each year, the annual report to the board of directors included the number of deaths among students and faculty. The report for the 1907–08 year told a sad story:

> On Wednesday night, February 19, John T. Shelton [senior in the preparatory department] . . . was in attendance upon the revival services [February Meetings]. . . . The next night, Thursday, the closing night of the meeting, he was ill. He grew worse, and his disease proved to be cerebro-spinal meningitis, the dread of even the advanced medical science of our times. The gravity of the disease had no effect on the volunteer nurses [students] unless it was to make them more anxious to serve. And noble service they rendered to the last.[9]

Students with contagious diseases were isolated, if possible, on one floor of a building. However, staff and students, busy with other duties, were not able to give the sick adequate attention. Meals were carried from the dining room, but the food was cold by the time it reached the sick. Finally, on May 26, 1908, the board of directors issued a directive:

Lamar Memorial Hospital

> The Board again expresses its very great solicitude that a College hospital be secured and the scientific care of the sick be provided for; and as a means of this end authorize Miss Henry, if she consent, to solicit funds towards such a hospital and its endowment, all expenses made necessary by her going to be paid from her collections or from the general treasury.[10]

Although Margaret was often called upon to raise funds for specific needs on campus, this request seemed a daunting task. About six months later, Martha Lamar (widow of Dr. Thomas Jefferson Lamar, professor of Greek language and literature and of sacred literature and second founder of the college) gave the needed $6,000 for a hospital in memory of her young son, Ralph Max, who had died in 1880 of meningitis. Margaret, then, began to raise funds for hospital equipment and for the salary of a full-time nurse. In a brief note to Major Cunningham she asked, "Do you know how many beds you are planning?"[11] The hospital was dedicated on May 4, 1910.

In a letter to Annie D. Robinson of Shadyside Presbyterian Church in Pittsburgh, Pennsylvania, Margaret wrote,

> I must tell you how grateful I am to you for your interest in the furnishing of the dining room of the Ralph Max Lamar Memorial Hospital. I shall not reach home until about the first of February, as the work has so piled up here. . . . I did want to be at home when the furniture comes so that I can have the joy of seeing it unpacked and put into place. I think I shall certainly have to take the first meal off the new table, sit in one of the chairs, and gaze with admiration at the sideboard, to say nothing of the loving interest in the rug. . . . [The dining room] has two big sunny windows and a glass door so that it is one of the most cheerful rooms in the hospital. What a pleasure it will mean to the convalescent students through all the future years. . . . I shall always be glad that our paths crossed, and you know that I am deeply grateful for your loving interest in the work which is so upon my heart.[12]

A few years later, Margaret reflected on the health of the student body in a letter to Mrs. Alexander Peacock, also from Shadyside Presbyterian, who had given a donation toward the salary of the nurse: "Last year we had ninety-five cases cared for in our Ralph Max Lamar Memorial Hospital, ranging from measles and mumps to typhoid and tetanus, and every life was saved."[13]

As the nurse became a beloved member of the community, Margaret reached out to many individuals and organizations for financial help:

> We are more and more pleased with our Canadian trained nurse, Miss Isabel MacLachlan. She is so capable and so interested in our boys and girls. . . . She seems to know how to do the right thing at the right time, radiates hope and cheer, and when the patients leave her, it is to be her loyal friends forever. . . . The nurse's salary is not so heavy a tax, since it is only $700 a year. I am hoping to find enough regular donors to give yearly toward

Miss MacLachlan's salary, to make it an assured fact from year to year.[14]

When faculty asked Margaret for financial help with a project, she turned to the president for permission. In a letter to Dr. Wilson, she wrote,

> It was Professor Gillingham's desire that while I am in the field, if possible, I should raise the funds for a projectoscope. I think that it is for use in his classes, as well as for the general use of the College. This projectoscope I believe will take any kind of a picture or post card and throw it upon the screen. I think the cost, including instrument and slides, is $250. . . . I find it impossible to plead persuasively for money that is not going to build into lives. . . . As our scholarship money this year amounts to more than it has any other year that I have been soliciting, I am perfectly willing that $250 of the money be applied toward the cost of the projectoscope, for I believe that it will be a broadening influence in the lives of our students.[15]

A few weeks later, Alice Gillingham, who was traveling with Margaret, wrote to her brother, Professor Clinton Gillingham: "I guess you will get your projectoscope all right. We sent the Major [Ben Cunningham, Treasurer] a check for $100 the other day. The donor, Mr. Charles Otis [Otis Elevators], did not designate it for a scholarship, so Miss Henry designated it for the projectoscope."[16]

In 1906, Margaret received a generous gift for student scholarships from the Central Congregational Church in West Newton, Massachusetts. In her letter of thanks to Mrs. Arthur P. Fenton, she answered questions and shared a bit of college history:

> Yes, indeed, many of our graduates enter the missionary field. In the last thirty years, [thirty-five] have gone to the Foreign Field, and a very much larger number have entered active mission work in the Home Field. Our College, while under the control of the

> Synod of the Presbyterian Church, is not narrow and sectarian. Its teachers are, and have been, of various denominations. Last year we had two hundred students who were Methodists and one hundred who were Baptists. The scholarships go to bright and worthy students irrespective of denomination. We seek in no [way] to make Presbyterians of them, but only to build them up into a noble Christian womanhood and manhood, well-equipped to take their part in life. . . . We have just had the dedicatory service of our beautiful new Elizabeth R. Voorhees Chapel—the gift of Mr. Ralph Voorhees, the blind philanthropist of Clinton, New Jersey. It is a tribute to his wife while she is yet living. Our first Chapel, eighty-seven years ago, was the little log sitting-room of the founder of the College, Rev. Isaac Anderson, D.D.; our second was a small Chapel in the antebellum college days which was barracks for the soldiers in the Civil War; our third, on the present College hill, was soon [outgrown], enlarged and [outgrown] again. [It was located on the second floor of Anderson Hall.] This beautiful new Chapel will not soon be [outgrown] for it will seat about one thousand students.[17]

Daily chapel services were held in Voorhees each day at 8:10 a.m., immediately after the first recitation hour. Margaret described the services to Mrs. James Flint of Weymouth, Massachusetts, who had donated Bibles to the college: "Various members of our faculty lead the morning devotions. We usually have a choir made up of about seventy-five of our students, under a musical director, and this delightful service of song adds greatly to the chapel exercises. At least once a week we have a short address upon some life topic of the times."[18]

Students were called to chapel by the ringing of the bell in the Anderson Hall tower. Each year, Margaret selected two or three responsible young men to raise the flag on the tower of Anderson each day and to share the responsibility of ringing the bell. Alice Gillingham

Voorhees Chapel

described their daily schedule to Rev. John Anderson in a letter she wrote for Margaret in January 1913.

> Three boys live in the "bell room" in Anderson Hall and are working out part of their expenses by ringing the college bell at regular intervals through the day from 6 a.m., the rising hour, until 10:30 p.m. for retiring. It must be rung for every meal, for chapel services, and to call the students to recitations every fifty-five minutes during the school hours. As all our work is done on schedule time, the boys must be punctual to the minute in performing this duty.[19]

In addition to Voorhees Chapel and Ralph Max Lamar Memorial Hospital, three other buildings were added to the campus plant during Margaret's tenure: Pearsons Hall (1910), Carnegie Hall (1910), and the Swimming Pool (1915). The original halls, Baldwin and Memorial, were forty years old in 1910, and newer accommodations for students were a pressing need. A monetary gift from Dr. Daniel K. Pearsons of Chicago enabled the construction of a two-story building that provided living

Pearsons Hall

space for thirty-four women plus parlors and meeting rooms for literary societies. Shortly after the hall opened, Margaret told a donor that Maude McMurray "is enjoying so much her room in the beautiful new Pearsons Hall in which the girls of the upper college classes have their home. In the October 'Cosmopolitan' there is a little article about Dr. Pearsons, the donor of this building. It seems that he helps only struggling colleges and has already given to forty-two or more."[20]

The Co-operative Boarding Club occupied the first floor of the hall; it included a dining room with a seating capacity of five hundred, a kitchen, offices, and waiting rooms. The cost to participate in the club was a modest $1.70 per week, up from $1.35 in 1903. As Margaret explained, "A New England lady systematized this department of our work many years ago, so that in spite of the increase in prices [for food], the cost to our students has gone up very slightly with the changing times. We have good wholesome meals, and our students thrive on them."[21]

As a contribution to the Forward Fund, Andrew Carnegie gave $50,000 toward a hall for young men. It had rooms to accommodate 108 students. Each of the two large wings provided a suite of rooms for

Carnegie Fire

a professor and his family. Six years later, while Margaret was working in New York City, Carnegie Hall was destroyed by a fire. In a letter to Elizabeth Patten of Middletown, Connecticut, Margaret shared the details:

> The boys worked bravely, trying to save the furniture. Those whose rooms were on the third floor lost all their personal property, and all the boys lost something. Two boys and two firemen were injured. . . . The fire occurred in the morning. That evening after supper, the students gathered in front of Dr. Wilson's home, singing the college songs and giving the college yells, until Dr. Wilson came out and gave them a talk. The moment he finished speaking, the entire student body began to sing, "God will take care of you." It was a great comfort to Dr. Wilson to have the young people show their sympathy in this way, and this shows you something of the spirit that prevails at Maryville.[22]

Swimming Pool Excavation

In 1915, a building was completed that housed a twenty-five-by-seventy-five-foot swimming pool. The student body, led by the YMCA cabinet, had started a movement a few years earlier for the construction of the pool. In a letter of thanks to Professor Albert P. Mills, who had sent a scholarship check to the college, Margaret shared this story:

> You may be interested to know that we are planning to open a splendid swimming pool for our students next term. Our students have had a noble share in this, for by real self denial and earnest effort in the past two years they have contributed $1,500 toward it. The total cost will be about $6,000, but this will be for the permanent good of our 800 students, for we try to do everything to safeguard their health and build them up

Pool and Bartlett Hall

> physically. We have football, baseball, basketball, a gymnasium, tennis courts, and physical directors for both boys and girls.[23]

Just as the campus physical plant was expanding with each new building, academic life was growing and changing also. Students were enrolled in either the College Department or the Preparatory Department. Other departments, such as Art, Teachers', and expression, were subsets of these two. When Margaret became scholarship secretary, the majors in the College Department led to one degree—a bachelor of arts. For two years, a bachelor of science degree was offered. During this time, the Preparatory Department was developing gradually. It had been added in 1866 following the Civil War to prepare students for college courses. In 1903, the department had three class levels: junior, middle, and senior. Then, in 1909, the structure changed significantly. Four class levels, similar to a high school, replaced the three levels. Specific requirements for graduation were established. A sub-preparatory class was added for those students who did not have the advantage of elementary training in their communities. Although most of Margaret's scholarship students were enrolled in the Preparatory Department, they were an integral part of the college. A catalog from this period of time states: "All privileges and advantages of the institution are available to students in the Preparatory Department."[24]

During the early years of Dr. Wilson's administration, three new departments were added: Bible Training (1907), Home Economics (1913), and Agricultural (1916). The Bible Training Department offered the study of the English Bible, Bible languages, and practical training for mission work. This department was well funded, which freed Margaret to tell prospective scholarship donors about the students preparing for missions both at home and abroad. The Home Economics Department prepared young women to return to their mountain communities with new knowledge and skills in food preparation and preservation, clothing, housekeeping, and home nursing. Margaret often referred to the new department as domestic science, as she did in this letter to Helen Sanborn of Boston:

> Through the generosity of a young woman from the West [Chicago], we have been able to add a Domestic Science Department this fall. The course is three years and will train our girls along very practical lines. The same donor granted us the money that made it possible . . . to add a third story to Fayerweather Science Hall, in order that the new Department might have suitable recitation rooms and laboratories.[25]

Margaret wanted a similar opportunity for the mountain boys, as she described in a letter to Mrs. Jasper Corning: "Since we have a campus of 235 acres, we do need an agricultural department because so many of our young men come from the country and need to be fitted to go back to the country and wring a living from the soil. We want domestic science and manual training departments to give our students work along practical lines."[26]

About six weeks before her premature death, Margaret wrote to a friend in Kennett Square, Pennsylvania, "that we have been able to begin the work of an Agricultural Department. About one hundred acres of the campus are to be devoted to this work. We have received a generous gift of money to build an up-to-date dairy barn, and other friends have donated valuable [livestock]."[27]

The Agricultural Department was discontinued in 1920 due to a lack of interest among the students; however, the dairy farm continued to provide milk for Maryville College students for another forty years. The other departments thrived and offered important majors in the academic program of the college.

On October 13, 1914, Margaret wrote to Mrs. George Scott, regent of the Chester County Chapter of the DAR in Philadelphia, Pennsylvania, about a very special event:

> In September our County Superintendent of Public Schools called us to a wonderful Educational Rally here on College Hill. The College authorities gave the Chapel for the occasion and there was a picnic dinner on our college campus. About fifteen hundred children and nearly two thousand people took part in the Rally and there were soul-stirring songs and addresses. All the rural school teachers in the vicinity of Maryville brought their entire body of school children to Maryville to take part in the Rally, each school having a separate banner and all uniting in patriotic songs. Every highway leading into Maryville on that day was alive with wagons, buggies and hacks, packed to the uttermost with happy, enthusiastic school children. It was a most inspiring occasion and one never to be forgotten by the children. Trissie [Whetsell] was here with all her happy school clan, and I wish that you could have seen the dignity with which she led them across our College campus, when they took their place with similar groups swelling the throng to fifteen hundred in number.[28]

The Chester County Chapter of the DAR had provided scholarships for Trissie Whetsell during the five years she was enrolled in the Preparatory Department at Maryville College. The members had taken a very personal interest in her by helping with incidental expenses and paying a dentist to have her teeth repaired and checked regularly.

With great happiness, Margaret watched many former students, like Trissie, return to the valleys to teach or to pursue other work. Margaret wrote,

> The educational awakening has come here in our Southern Mountains, and each student going back to his home community from our College has been an influence, inspiring other young people to desire a college education. The teachers of the mountain academies have written us, asking us to make a way for their most promising students to come to Maryville College.[29]

In 1892, Jasper Barnes (later Dr. Barnes) joined the faculty as principal of the Preparatory Department and professor of the science and art of teaching. Prior to the arrival of Dr. Barnes and until 1897, the college had no formal teacher education program. Most of the teachers in the mountain valleys had attended the Preparatory Department for one or perhaps two years. In 1897, Dr. Barnes established the Teachers' Department, which offered a five-year course of study beginning with the first year in the Preparatory Department. It included three courses in pedagogy. By 1910, the department was offering a six-year program, four years in the Preparatory Department and two in the College Department. Students who completed the six years had the option of taking two additional years of work to graduate from Maryville College in the Education Group of studies and receive a bachelor's degree. Professional courses included the following:

- Three courses in pedagogy (School Management and Methods of Teaching I and II)
- Psychology Applied to Education
- History of Education
- Genetic Psychology

- Educational Psychology

Margaret was grateful that efforts were made to accommodate students who returned in the winter term after teaching in the settlement schools during the fall term. The catalog described the plan:

> [S]pecial courses in history, civics, higher arithmetic, and grammar are offered. For example, Normal English Grammar is a course based on an extensive study of Technical English grammar. The subject is presented from the teacher's standpoint, methods of teaching are discussed, and each member of the class is required, at times, to take his turn in conducting the recitation . . . . Special double courses in Beginning Latin and Beginning Algebra are provided, by which a full year's credit . . . may be secured during the winter and spring terms. The classes recite ten hours each week, and prepare respectively for Caesar and Advanced Algebra.[30]

While on the wing, Margaret was very grateful for the support she received from the faculty at the college. They monitored students' academic progress, distributed gifts, handled behavioral problems, and assisted Margaret in countless ways. Alice Clemens, an English teacher in the Preparatory Department, often helped scholarship students write letters. In the spring of 1912, Margaret asked Alice to help Zenie Henry write a thank-you letter. Zenie was a new student in the Preparatory Department.

> Now I am writing to ask a favor of you. I know that Zenie Henry is untutored and perhaps will not know how to write a thank-you letter. I have interested two organizations in her and I want her to write a letter to each. The letters can be exactly the same. Will you help Zenie on these two letters? Have her make them as full and interesting as possible about herself, her college work, and her appreciation of the college help.[31]

Occasionally Margaret met a scholarship student who was related to one of her classmates from the 1870s. She described John F. Parker of Louisville, Tennessee, to Mrs. W. K. Porter as

> a rosy-cheeked lad, so fond of athletics, so willing to work to help meet his incidental expenses, and so earnest in his class room work, that it is a joy to feel that he will make one of the practical workers of the world. His younger sister, Helen, is in college this year, and is being educated by a lady who grants her scholarship as a memorial to her little daughter who died nearly forty years ago. John is named after an uncle who was a classmate of mine in college. He often reminds me of this uncle in many of his characteristics. The uncle, Dr. John Heron, was a medical missionary to Korea and lost his life there [in 1890] when the cholera plague was raging, by trying to save the lives of the natives through that dread summer.[32]

Over the years, Margaret stayed in close contact with a former classmate, Mrs. Edward (Anne) Sudbury of Mount Vernon, New York. The good friends exchanged letters regularly, and Margaret visited with Anne when she was traveling in the Northeast. Like typical alumnae, they talked about college life and the faculty of the 1870s. Anne, in particular, found Dr. Peter Mason Bartlett, president and professor of mental and moral science, to be an outstanding teacher. For that reason, she wrote to Dr. Wilson and other college leaders in 1908 to suggest that a plaque be placed in Voorhees Chapel in memory of Dr. Bartlett. The commencement program for June 2, 1909, shows that a memorial service was held following the commencement exercises entitled, "Unveiling of a Tablet to the memory of Rev. Peter Mason Bartlett, D.D., President of Maryville College from 1869 until 1887."[33]

Three days after commencement, Margaret wrote to Anne:

> I went over to the Memorial Service to see the unveiling of the beautiful bronze tablet for which you labored so many, many long months and wrote such a multitude of letters. It is

> perfect in design and finish, and you deserve a memorial tablet yourself for pushing matters so gently and yet so persistently that the work which Rev. Bartlett wrought in our lives in other days may be recalled by this tangible tribute to his memory. Then, too, the younger generation who knew him not, need to know that Dr. Bartlett, Professor Lamar [Dr. Thomas Jefferson Lamar], and Professor Alexander Bartlett, [professor of Latin language and literature] laid foundations on which others could build more easily. . . . Dr. Elmore, Class of 1874 [Dr. Edgar Alonzo Elmore, D.D., pastor of the Second Presbyterian Church, Chattanooga, Tennessee] gave the memorial address. I am sure you do not forget what an impressive speaker he is, and this time it was not the impressiveness of mere oratory, but that of deep feeling.[34]

Margaret was pleased when Rev. William Thaw Bartlett, Class of 1901, son of Dr. Peter Mason Bartlett and pastor of Katonah Presbyterian Church of Katonah, New York, invited her to speak at his church. In a letter to Rev. Bartlett's widowed mother she wrote,

> I had such a happy little visit over Sunday with your son and daughter. They have such a comfortable manse, such a pretty stone church and such fine people to work among. . . . You will be glad to know that Mr. Bartlett's people granted two scholarships of $50 each to Maryville College. Wasn't that splendid! I had the morning and evening service in the church. In the morning I told them of the College, and what a part Dr. Bartlett, Professor Lamar, and Professor Bartlett played in the reorganization of the College after the Civil War.[35]

The general membership of Katonah Presbyterian Church gave the first scholarship. The second came from the children of W. W. Snyder. A letter written by the children to Rev. Bartlett reads,

Dear Mr. Bartlett,

We were very glad to hear about Maryville College, and learn why you love the Southland so much.

Our father says that we five little ones may give a scholarship of $50 if our Church will make up enough to make complete the other scholarship.

With love to you and Mrs. Bartlett from Helen, Wallace, Andrus, Gretchen and Edward[36]

Margaret wrote a letter of thanks to the children and told them about the student receiving their scholarship: Martha Roberts from Cades Cove.

Another beloved faculty member during the 1870s and 1880s was Professor Gideon Stebbins White Crawford, class of 1871, who taught mathematics. He was a member of the first postbellum class, which enrolled on September 5, 1866. Gideon completed his theological studies at Lane Seminary in 1874, returned home immediately to marry Jennie Duncan, and started teaching at Maryville College in the fall. A few years later, the young couple built a new home on the southeastern edge of the campus, near the residence of Dr. Thomas Jefferson Lamar. Gideon died in 1891 at the age of forty one. He left behind a young widow and six children. All the children attended Maryville College, and five graduated. In 1899, the two youngest of the Crawford children entered the Preparatory Department: Jennie Firdilla, twelve years old and Samuel Earle, nine years old. After Margaret began the scholarship work in 1903, she found scholarships for the two children. In 1906 she wrote to Edna Bowker of Brookline, Massachusetts, about Jennie's progress: "She is very domestic, and a great help and comfort to her mother. . . . Jennie is nineteen years old, and in the freshman class. . . . She is a most earnest and faithful student."[37] Jennie graduated in 1911 and became a teacher and later the principal of Fort Craig School in Maryville.

Gideon's youngest child, Samuel Earle, was a gifted athlete, which occasionally got in the way of his schoolwork. Margaret told Sarah E. Lamb in 1906 that

> he is such a bright handsome boy. Although he has not applied himself with the same earnestness that his older brothers showed yet we are hoping to see him again with each year, for he is naturally bright. He has had his first taste of football in a boys' team, and that has interfered somewhat with his highest mental development, because he has lacked the age in [judgment] to balance work and play properly.[38]

Samuel Earle graduated in 1912. He was president of the senior class and the quarterback on the football team. He was a dentist in Maryville for sixty years and lived in the Crawford home on the campus. (The Mountain Challenge program is currently located in Crawford House.)

Although Margaret's fund-raising efforts focused on the financial needs of the children from the Southern Mountains, she also found scholarships for needy students from elsewhere in the United States and many foreign countries. In a letter to Mrs. R. D. Dudley, Margaret wrote, "You may wonder how these foreign students ever learn of our college, so far away in this Southland. In the last thirty years Maryville College has sent thirty-five missionaries into the foreign field, and thrice that number into the home field. It is through these workers that the foreign students often hear of us."[39]

Six Maryville College missionaries serving in Siam (now called Thailand) in 1906 met a young Japanese youth, Oki Mori, and encouraged him to enroll at Maryville College. After Oki arrived on campus, Margaret wrote to the Missionary Society of Bryn Mawr Presbyterian Church of Haverford, Pennsylvania, and shared his story:

> Through their influence he came to Maryville College, for they assured him that a way would be made for him here even if he did not have the money. . . . Oki is one of my pupils and I assure you that he is a most faithful one. He is trying his very best to grasp every subject, although he has a very small command of language. He understands almost all that is said to him, and he can write very well indeed.[40]

Ernest Chalmers Brown

Faculty and staff were always pleased to receive letters from alumni. In May 1915, Dr. Wilson heard from James A. Burnett, an attorney, in Asheville, North Carolina. James, who had graduated from the Preparatory Department in 1910, wrote,

> I have been wanting to write you a letter for some time. It has been a long time since I was at Maryville, still I never cease to remember the dear old school. I finished my course at the University and got a law license the first day of February and have been practicing since then. I am going to work hard and try to make good. The older I grow, the more appreciative I become of the teachings received at dear old Maryville. There the teaching of character building combined with a Christ-like spirit establish a life that will last when all else is gone. And I am sure that a worthy student will never appeal in vain to the people of Maryville for help or encouragement. I hope the school may

Eula McCurry

> grow stronger, prosper and uphold the record of the glorious past. Give my best regards to the members of the faculty that I know and the students that were with me there. Hoping you and all at Maryville many, many years of continued success.[41]

Several of Margaret's students became outstanding faculty and staff members during the twentieth century. Two young men, Ernest Chalmers Brown ("Brownie") of Maryville and Eula Erskine McCurry (later known as "Mr. Mac") of Mosheim, entered the Preparatory Department in 1903 and 1905, respectively. Brownie was a seventh grader in Margaret's English class. He joined the campus crew in 1910 and was named the college engineer in 1916, a position he held until his retirement in 1961. Eula McCurry received a scholarship from Margaret and earned money for board and incidentals by ringing the college bell and carrying the mail.

Edgar Walker

Margaret described Eula as a very dependable young man to Mrs. J. W. Reisner:

> Promptness is one of his chief characteristics, as well as faithfulness to duty. He carries the college mail back and forth between College Hill and the post office, three times a day. Only the most dependable students are given this work. Although it is half a mile from the College to the post office, he makes the trip in an incredibly short time, and plans his going so as not to interfere with any of his classes. I often think that Eula is the happiest boy we have in college. He is like one who has come out from the shadow of the mountains into the sunshine.[42]

Mr. Mac was the proctor of Carnegie Hall from 1920 until 1959. He earned a bachelor of arts degree in 1934.

Augustus Sisk

Professor Edgar Roy Walker, who taught mathematics and physics from 1909 to 1955, enrolled in the Preparatory Department in 1901. He received a yearly scholarship from the Missionary Society of the Kenwood Evangelical Church of Chicago, Illinois. In a letter to a society member, Margaret wrote,

> He is such a bright boy. He lives on a little farm near the mountains in East Tennessee. His father and mother work early and late in the home, and though there are four or five children, Edgar is the only one so far who has seemed to care for a college education. He is an all-round student, doing more work than any other student to help himself financially in college. He has work in the dining room of the Co-operative Dining Club [Co-operative Boarding Club] and also in the library.[43]

Edwin Hunter

Edgar graduated in 1909 and began teaching mathematics in the Preparatory Department. A few years later he married a local girl. The young couple lived in the faculty apartment of Carnegie Hall. During that time, their first child, Arda Susan, was born. A generation of Maryville College history majors will remember with appreciation Dr. Arda Walker, class of 1940, who served her college well from 1948 until 1985.

In May 1916, Margaret wrote a letter of thanks to Mrs. Frank Lebar of Overbrook, Pennsylvania, for a scholarship assigned to Augustus Sisk from Marion, North Carolina: "[He] will be a Junior next year in the college department. He is an excellent student, and the reports that have come to me show that his grades have been high."[44] Dr. Sisk, class of 1917, returned to the college in 1938 as professor of mathematics and physics.

Edwin Ray Hunter from Carlyle, Illinois, who enrolled at Maryville College in 1911, was an outstanding student. Margaret's letters to Edwin's scholarship donor, F. C. Gustetter of Cincinnati, Ohio, spoke of a bright future for the young man: "Your scholarship student, Edwin Ray Hunter, age 22, is now a junior, and has made a splendid record in college this year. I hope you will soon have a letter from him that can be read to your Sunday School. . . . I cannot help but feel that he will be able to accomplish much for the good of the world."[45] Students enrolled between 1918 and 1967 will remember Dr. Edwin R. Hunter, class of 1914: dean of curriculum, professor of English, chair of the English department, poet, and author of scholarly works on Chaucer, Shakespere (spelling preferred by Dr. Hunter) and Faulkner.

Mary Miles enrolled in the Preparatory Department in 1912. Her father, Thomas Judson Miles, had graduated in 1893 and was a pastor in Knoxville. In a letter to a prospective donor, Margaret shared the family's situation:

> Mary belongs to a family of five children, and her father and mother are in very limited circumstances. They have charge of a small country church on the small salary of $800. Out of this, they give $100 back into the church treasury, and it is only by the very closest economy that they are able to live. The parents are such fine people; they did not ask scholarship help for Mary and her sister Emma, but we were anxious to have them in college and offered to grant them scholarships. . . . Mary is only sixteen years old. She works in the dining room of the Co-operative Club waiting on tables, to help meet her board bill. She comes to us well recommended, with splendid grades, all ranging above 90. I feel that she will remain in college until she graduates and that she will be an honor to our institution and a joy to all of us.[46]

As Margaret predicted, Mary excelled academically. She participated in musical groups and was an assistant in the Piano Department during her senior year. Following graduation in 1918, Mary, who had majored in modern languages, prepared to go abroad as a missionary. From 1920 until 1940 she taught music at a girl's high school in Kanazawa, Japan. When World War II broke out, Mary was home on furlough.

She returned to Maryville College in 1948 as an assistant in the library. Following the retirement of Clemmie Henry (Margaret's successor), Mary became the student-help secretary in 1952 and the director of student help in 1957. She retired in 1966. Margaret Henry, Clemmie Henry, and Mary Miles enabled several generations of students to attend Maryville College between 1903 and 1966.

Margaret witnessed many changes in her dear old college during the thirteen years she served as scholarship secretary. As she traveled for nine months in the Northeast during that last year, her letters were filled with joy about an enrollment of more than eight hundred students, a 250-acre campus with fifteen buildings, a strong student-help program, and an excellent Teachers' Department. By June 1, she had raised money for three hundred scholarships and increased the endowed scholarship program. Over the years, her reputation as a successful fund-raiser and gifted spokeswoman for this small liberal arts college became known by many colleges and organizations. As a result, she received numerous job offers with higher salaries and less travel, but her answer to each was always the same: "As my interests have been interwoven with the work of this institution for more than a score of years, it will be impossible for me to consider any other opening so long as I can serve Maryville College."[47]

And serve she did.

January 21st, 1911.

Miss Faith A. Ingraham,
Treas. Katherine Gaylord Chapter D.A.R.,
Bristol, Connecticut.

My dear Miss Ingraham:

Our college treasurer, Major Ben Cunningham, has just handed me your letter of recent date, together with receipts for the two scholarships coming to us from the Katherine Gaylord Chapter D. A. R. I am forwarding the receipts to you.

These will be applied to the education of Tallahassie Coulter, who has the Lena Josephine Upson Memorial Scholarship granted by Miss Ella A. Upson, and to Daisy Morton, who now has your scholarship in the absence of Josie Weisgerber, who is still at home with her poor, suffering sister.

You will be interested to know that we have just dedicated Carnegie Hall, our beautiful new dormitory for the boys of the College. It is the gift of Mr. Andrew Carnegie, and will accommodate one hundred and eight boys. It also has two suites of rooms for professors' families. I enclose a program of the dedicatory exercises. The Rev. Dr. Elmore, President of the Board of Directors, who formally received the building, entered Maryville College in the poverty-stricken days just after the Civil War. He could indeed speak most feelingly of the growth and progress of the College during these intervening years.

With deep gratitude for your continued interest in the scholarship work of Maryville College, I am
Sincerely yours,

A Growing Campus

I want these young people educated and turned back to their home communities . . . to become a force for good in the world's best work.

—Margaret E. Henry

CHAPTER FOUR

Scholarships for Mountain Boys and Mountain Girls

In 1902, Mrs. Charles A. (Angie Warren) Perkins, a member of Ossoli Circle in Knoxville (the oldest federated women's club in the South), learned that Margaret had been offered the position of scholarship secretary at Maryville College. To encourage her to accept the call, Mrs. Perkins wrote a letter of introduction for Margaret to carry during her travels. Mrs. Perkins was a member of the board of directors of the General Federation of Women's Clubs and had many friends throughout the Northeast.

> To Any One Interested in the Mountain [Students] of the South:
>
> It gives me great pleasure to be the means of making you acquainted with Miss Margaret E. Henry, the bearer of this note, but a resident of Maryville, Tennessee, where she has lived for many years, her father having resided in the mountainous region of this part of the State. In fact, he was a mountaineer himself and possessed those sterling qualities which are making of his people the bone and sinew of Eastern Tennessee.
>
> And as Miss Henry pleads for these children of the hills and coves, she knows whereof she speaks. She is a teacher in Maryville

Miss Margaret

College, where she graduated, and where, today many of the children of the mountains are receiving their education.

Miss Henry was Secretary of the State Federation and has accomplished much in establishing schools in these mountain vastnesses where the children had no school privileges. In her early womanhood she went to Japan as a missionary, but a fall on the steamer incapacitated her for work and she was obliged to return to her native land, where she found among the mountains of Tennessee, a field that was ripe for the harvest, though the laborers were few.

I trust that you can do something to aid Miss Henry in her good work, and by so doing the blessing of heaven will come to you and to the children of the mountains.[1]

And so began Margaret's journey. She recounted her first trip north in a letter to Mrs. Frederick A. Strong of the Federated Women's Club of Bridgeport, Connecticut:

> The Year of Grace 1903, on a chilled November day, I was sitting in my room in a New York hotel, wondering whether in all that big Northland, I would ever be able to raise any money for the Scholarship Fund and Maryville College. As I had just started out in the work of collecting this fund, and as few organizations had given me a hearing, I was very much discouraged. Just at this juncture my mail was brought in, and I broke the seal on a letter from you, and to my great joy it contained the check which was the first to come in, and laid the foundation of the Scholarship Fund of Maryville College.[2]

Each spring, Margaret wrote to federated women's clubs, DAR chapters, churches, colleges, and other organizations to schedule speaking engagements for the next year. Her requests were few: "My terms [to speak] are simply a hearing and my railroad fare to and from my headquarters in the city."[3]

Before a program began, she usually requested a cup of coffee and a slice of bread and butter. Margaret was a gifted speaker. As one friend commented shortly after her death, "We did not hear about [the mountain people] but we met them, saw them, talked with them, heard their quaint Southern speech, and felt that we had always known them."[4]

After each speech, Margaret hoped for a pledge of $50 to the Scholarship Fund for a current student or a new applicant. This amount covered tuition and a room in the dormitory for a year. Scholarship students were assigned student-help jobs on campus in order to pay for their monthly board fee and to purchase incidentals. Many were employed as waiters and assistants in the dining room. Others worked in various places: janitors in buildings, groundskeepers, helpers in the library, or assistants in offices and labs.

Although the families of these students were generally very poor, they were urged to make a small contribution toward the board fee or for incidentals. As Margaret explained, "We think that it is best for them to put forth some effort [on] behalf of their children so that they will appreciate what is being done for them."[5] During Margaret's tenure, expenses at Maryville College were moderate. Tuition was $18 per year and board ranged from $1.35 per week in 1903 to $1.90 in 1915.

Whether on the road or at home, Margaret spent several hours each day writing to donors, telling them about the academic progress, daily life, and needs of individual students. When a benefactor had a personal interest in a student, the possibility of a renewed scholarship at the end of the year was greater.

Margaret encouraged the Women's Guild of North Presbyterian Church of Buffalo, New York, to renew the scholarship for Herman L. Caton from Cosby. "He is now a Sophomore, and you may know that he is worthy of your help when I tell you that last year his class standing was 'A,' which means that he graded above 90 in every study. Herman is very ambitious and wishes to fit himself for a professorship in some institution of learning and inclines toward the chair of Latin."[6]

Margaret began working with mountain children two years before she became scholarship secretary. In 1901, the Tennessee State Federation of Women's Clubs, under the leadership of Mrs. Charles A. Perkins, president, voted to begin a project to combat illiteracy in the Southern Mountains. Margaret, a member of the Chilhowee and Tuesday Clubs of Maryville, was appointed chairman. About the same time, Black Bill Walker, the patriarch of a remote mountain cove twenty-five miles from Maryville, requested a school for his valley, where eight families with approximately thirty children lived. Margaret and a crew of workers responded to the call. To reach the valley, located on the West Prong of Little River between Fodderstack Mountain and Lumber Ridge, they had to travel for two days and one night. Early the next morning, Black Bill and other men from the valley helped the volunteers repair an old log cabin, which became the first schoolhouse.

Black Bill and Nancy Walker

Walker Valley School operated for two months during the summer of 1902 with excellent results. The women of the federation continued to support the school with finances and their presence. Several years later, in a thank-you note to Clara Quinby of New Jersey for a $50 scholarship for Lillie Stinnett of Walker Valley, Margaret wrote,

> A great deal has been done by the club women of Tennessee for the improvement of this valley, not only in caring for the Settlement School there in the summer, but also in improving the schoolhouse itself. It has had a new floor, ceiling, roof, windows and doors. One of my former pupils, who now has a planing mill, gave me twenty-four desks for the schoolhouse. . . . The people have put a fence about the yard, with gates, in order to keep the

Walker Valley School

> stock out, and there are many, many things to encourage us in the valley. . . . After our work was carried there, the people put a fence around the little graveyard lying on the mountain slope. Then they began to care for the graves, to cover them with flowers and ferns. One of our valley students who had become a teacher, bought the first tombstones that were ever in the valley, and put them up to the graves of her brother and sister.[7]

Although the federation adopted other settlement schools in Greenbrier, Mountain Dale, Elkmont, and Rocky Branch, Margaret always had a special affinity for the children of Walker Valley. She encouraged them to look for educational opportunities beyond their mountain community. Dora Stinnett, the oldest daughter of Moll Stinnett (the third wife of Black Bill Walker) enrolled in the Junior Preparatory Department at Maryville College in 1906. Over the next six years, three sisters followed her lead. After mastering

Stinnett Family

the basic classes, Dora, who proved to be a committed and conscientious student, entered the teachers' program, which she completed successfully in 1914.

Like most mountain people, Dora had a strong sense of family and looked for ways to help her mother and siblings. Margaret shared this story with Dora's benefactor:

Dewberry the Ox

> [She] has had her brothers hauling lumber up the mountain trail with the sled and Old Dewberry, the ox, to add at least two new rooms to their home, and her ambition is also to add windows and a porch. I am glad that you are so generous and judge Dora, not by your standards of courtesies of life, but by the standards of one to the mountains born. When you remember that there have been several generations in Dora's family unable to read and write, I think that you will understand why she has not always remembered to answer your kindly letters and postcards as promptly as she should. She is a girl of much beauty of character as well as personal charm. She is the soul of gentleness and very refined in her manners. I feel deep joy in that your mother's memorial scholarship is building into such a life.[8]

In 1907, Dora's sister Lillie enrolled in the Preparatory Department, followed by Millie and Sallie Ann in 1911. Dora felt responsible for the

Dora and Lillie Stinnett

younger girls. Twice during her eight years at the college, she withdrew for the fall semester to work so she could help them with incidental expenses.

Millie worked in the dining room of the Co-operative Boarding Club. Margaret saw her at work in the spring of that first year: "I looked at Millie at dinnertime today, as she waited on the table, and I thought it would do your hearts good to see how she has developed and what a lovely, graceful girl she is, as she moves about her work in the dining room. She is not quite so bright as her sister Sallie Ann, but she does have grit and grace and perseverance."[9]

Two years later, Millie was given added responsibility, as Margaret described in this letter:

> Millie's special task in the dining room is to collect all the slices of bread left on the tables after meals in order that they may be toasted for breakfast, and also to care for the bread-

> cutting table in the pantry. This table has a modern bread-cutting machine attached to it, which cuts up loaf after loaf for a host of hungry young people. More than 500 students board at this Co-operative Club.[10]

Sallie Ann was the brightest and most athletic of the four sisters. She, too, worked in the dining room, and she also held the position of lifeguard on the days when the girls used the pool. Sallie received a scholarship from Maude Battelle Warren of Dorchester, Massachusetts. Margaret was delighted to tell Mrs. Warren about Sallie:

> [She] now signs herself "Sarah" Stinnett and she has taken on a good deal of dignity with the new name. She seems to have passed completely out of childhood. She is so tall, slender and serious looking though no doubt she can be funny enough when she is off duty. She is now seventeen years old and is one of our most athletic girls. She is an expert swimmer, a tireless walker, and a famous mountain climber. A friend of mine visited in her valley last summer and tells me that Sarah can swim with ease across the river that rolls in front of her door and back to the other bank without stopping. She can climb to the top of a great boulder in the river and slide off into the dark pool of water twelve feet deep, swim under water and come out at a point far distant from the boulder. She has perfect poise, mental and physical, due to her free life in the open in her beautiful mountain valley. She has known what it is to toil in the cornfields on the steep mountain slope from dewy morn to dewy eve. She has known what it is to jump from boulder to boulder across the swift current of Little River. She has walked with fearless tread, with bare feet, close to a rattlesnake's den. She has killed water moccasins and copperheads. She has been close to the haunts of wildcats, bear and deer. She has scaled the dizzy height of the forest trees of the Big Smoky Mountains, and now with equal

Stinnett Cabin

> ease she is scaling the heights of her college subjects and always manages to keep ahead.
>
> I am glad that you are going to remember her at the Christmastide. How would you like to send her a wonder-bag, full of many little gifts carefully tied up so she can have the joy of undoing them? I suggest a few articles that would delight Sarah's heart, a fancy turn over collar, a good story book, stationery and a few stamps for home letters, a fountain pen, toilet articles, a box of candy, handkerchiefs, and a few ribbons.[11]

Margaret took a personal interest in the lives of all the scholarship students. Her letters reveal that she understood their hearts and knew their needs. In the winter of 1914, she sent a gift of $5 to Dora Stinnett and suggested that she purchase a dress for her mother and go home for a few days. When a donor wanted to send a gift to a specific student, Margaret responded immediately with suggestions of appropriate clothing (including sizes), incidentals, and meaningful keepsakes. She reminded students to write thank-you notes promptly and often checked the notes before they were mailed. When Mrs. F. W. Brode of Memphis sent a $5 check to Caddie James, Margaret took Caddie to the bank to endorse and cash the check. This was followed by a trip to the dry-goods store to purchase a pair of shoes, stockings, and galoshes. As Margaret wrote to Mrs. Brode, "I want to develop her along business lines. She has had so little money in her life that it is altogether a new experience to be allowed to spend such a vast sum as $5."[12]

Foremost in Margaret's mind and heart was the health of each student. She scheduled dental appointments, arranged eye examinations, and found the means to pay the doctors. Like a good mother, she urged the girls, in particular, to rest more or to enjoy sunshine and fresh air. And for Mae Swanner, she purchased a new crutch.

Mae came to Maryville College in 1902 from Meadow, a small community on the eastern edge of Loudon County. Over the course of eleven years and against tremendous odds, Mae graduated with a bachelor of arts degree from the College Department in 1913. In a letter to Dr. and Mrs. J. T. Kerr, leaders in the Third Presbyterian Church of Elizabeth, New Jersey, Margaret described her first memory of Mae:

> An ignorant country doctor, in Mae's infancy, prescribed a powerful remedy for weak muscles, which made her lose the use of one side of her body. The first time I ever saw her, standing beside me on the roughest, old, [homemade] crutch, with features that looked almost blank and hopeless, a pang went through my heart because of the hopelessness of her ever trying to aspire to an education. She has lived to prove to me that these fears were altogether without grounds, for she has made very high grades and has really been almost a leader among the girls along the various lines of work, especially literary and religious.[13]

Mae's mother was an invalid. While milking one summer, the cow's tail, which contained cockleburs, struck her in the eye and injured the lid. Cancer developed, and her eye and part of the lid had to be removed. During this same time, Mae's father lost his store to a fire. As her mother's health deteriorated, Mae withdrew from school to care for her and the younger children. Margaret wrote a letter of support and encouragement:

> Though you have not written me about it, I am sure that your heart was heavy in September because you could not come back to college. You will keep a brave heart and a sunny face before your mother and hide from her your disappointment. I feel that this term in your life will not be truly lost. Either it is meant to build you up in the grace of unselfishness and in a deepening of your faith, or it is meant to build you up in health. I know that there is something in it for you and that you will look back upon it after many years and say "It is well." Whenever I pass your room at Baldwin I think of you. Indeed, I have thought of you every day since College opened. Be as brave as you can, remembering how much your mother has to bear.[14]

After the death of her mother, Mae returned to school in the fall of 1910. She carried a heavy class load and attended summer terms to catch up on the work she had missed. The Norwalk Chapter of the DAR in Darien, Connecticut, gave a scholarship for Mae's tuition and room rent. Small gifts from the auxiliaries of several churches provided funds for board and incidentals. Margaret wrote, "We have never had a student who appreciated more deeply than Mae the help that has been granted her. She expresses it to us frequently in words, and proves it always in her splendid work."[15]

Although Mae was not able to do heavy work on campus, Margaret wrote about her many kindnesses to other students. In one letter she wrote, "She is doing good as she goes along here in college, for she comforts many a homesick girl. She guides many a thoughtless, wayward girl, and she makes others feel what the life of a conscientious, faithful, hard-working student stands for."[16] In another letter, she wrote, "Mae . . . is beloved by all the girls in the hall. She is especially fine in outlining talks or addresses, and she is a great help to the girls who have to speak in their literary societies or YWCA, as she helps them prepare their address."[17] No doubt Margaret and the students missed Mae after she graduated and started teaching in a small rural school.

In 1909, the College passed a new rule stating that no boarding student would be admitted who was under the age of fifteen. Currently enrolled students under fifteen had to move into homes in the community. Brother and sister Hugh (Elijah Elihu) and Caddie (Cadelle) James struggled to afford the higher cost of living off-campus. They came from a little farm, which their parents rented, near the foothills of the Great Smoky Mountains. There were several children in the family, all very close in age, and Margaret described them as "little stair-steps" when she wrote about their situation:

> [The parents] have been in very limited circumstances this year on account of the little baby that has kept the mother from doing as much marketing as usual. It is the mother in this home who has the push and energy and makes things move for the good of her family. The father is slow and timid and rather content with what he has. It is the mother who aspires to an education for her children.[18]

Hugh was enrolled from 1907 until he graduated from the Preparatory Department in 1916. Caddie entered the Junior Preparatory class in 1907 and remained in school until 1912.

For several years, Grace Cleveland Porter of Summit, New Jersey, gave a scholarship for Hugh. She was always eager to receive word about his life on the campus. In one letter, Margaret wrote,

> Hugh is here, one of the smallest boys in College, and also one of the youngest. He works so hard in the field during the vacation days that he always comes back to us looking gaunt and thin, with those big gray eyes of his having the look of an old man in them. It does not take very many meals at the Co-operative Club, or very much recreation on the campus, to

> bring the roses back to his cheeks and the sunny look of youth back to his face.[19]

In another letter, Margaret told of Hugh's academic progress, his off-campus home, and his work-study job:

> I am sending you the official statement of Hugh James' standing as a student in Maryville College. "B Plus" means that he has averaged above 86. If you could see the little mite of a fellow you would wonder that he could make grades quite so high. He works on the campus every afternoon, and I wish you could see him. The boys have been preparing the soil for a hedge, and Hugh has trundled wheelbarrows full of good soil up to the hedge like a little man. Sometimes he empties the [paper boxes] that are on the campus, and trundles the papers away in a wheelbarrow to be burned. The other day I took a walk near our college grove, and he was piling brush on a big [bonfire] where the boys were clearing the forest. His cheeks were red and rosy and his eyes were as bright as stars. Mrs. [Emilie] Webb, the dear lady in whose home he stays, is very fond of him. She looks after him so well. She is interested not only in his wardrobe, but in his health and every detail of his college work.[20]

Hugh's sister, Caddie, was fourteen when the boarding rule was added. Margaret took Caddie into her own home for the year until she was old enough to move back to Baldwin Hall. Caddie proved to be a delightful visitor and willing to help with household work. When Margaret found that Caddie had few clothes because her mother, who worked daily in the fields, knew very little about sewing, she asked Mrs. F. W. Brode of Memphis to consider sending a box of dresses plus stockings, soap, a toothbrush, and a comb and brush. Later, in a letter of thanks, she described Caddie's delight: "I had the pleasure of going through the package with Caddie, and I never saw a child so happy and so delighted as she was with everything. I am having some of the dresses altered to fit her. Caddie has grown to be a really beautiful girl. . . . I am enclosing a little letter from her to you, which will tell you in part how much she appreciates your gift."[21]

Margaret found that many young men carried such heavy burdens at home, they were not able to enter the college at a young age. Sadly, those students felt compelled to withdraw after a short time in school to work and help their families survive. Otha Abraham Gibson was eighteen when he entered the first year of the Preparatory Department. Margaret described him to a member of the Young Peoples' Association of Orange, New Jersey:

> Otha is much stronger than when he first came to college. I think the family was so poor that he and Mae [his sister] scarcely had enough to eat, and they just looked pale and hungry. Since Otha takes his meals at the Co-operative Club of the College, which furnishes good, wholesome food at $6.80 a month, he looks like a different boy. I do not believe there is a college anywhere in the south that furnishes such splendid fare at such low rates. For even here in the south the cost of living has gone up, while the lady in charge of the Club has worked earnestly to keep the price of board down. I take most of my meals at the Club. Perhaps you would be interested to know the menu for today. There was roast beef with gravy, corn bread, light bread, beans, mashed Irish potatoes, slaw, and delicious apples for dessert.
>
> Otha is doing splendid work in his classes. He also has work on the campus to help meet his incidental expenses. I feel sure that he will work this summer . . . for he needs all the money he can earn through the vacation to use toward his expenses in college.
>
> Otha's English teacher told me today that she had demanded rather lengthy written work for the daily recitation, and called upon her pupils to read what they had written. Otha's paper was very well prepared, but as he began to read, stage fright struck him very hard. He grew pale and his voice utterly failed him, and

> he sank down into his desk. The teacher said, "If you can do so, you may read the remainder of the paper sitting down at your desk." He answered very promptly, "No, I am not going to give up." And with tremendous will power he rose, stood facing the class, and read his paper through from beginning to end, feeling that he had gotten the victory in so doing. When he sat down after this, he had to mop the perspiration from his brow, but he had conquered.[22]

After two years in school, Otha withdrew and went to work to help support his family and to enable his younger brothers and sisters to attend college.

Margaret found that students enrolled in the teachers' program of study, added in 1897 to the Preparatory Department, required her constant attention. Often, students who came from small rural schools enrolled in the new program for a few terms to complete the basic courses. Then they withdrew for a fall term to teach and to save money. Rural schools opened in summer after the planting season and closed at harvest time. This schedule enabled former students to re-enroll in the teachers' course at Maryville College for the winter and spring terms. Course schedules were adjusted for teachers. For example, a section of a course typically taught in the fall might be added in the spring. Also, many review courses were offered for teachers who returned to the college for the winter or spring terms. Margaret stayed in touch with the students who had withdrawn, encouraged them to return, and helped with the scheduling of needed courses. When they returned in the winter, often a younger brother or sister came along. Margaret had to scramble to find a scholarship, but she never turned a child away.

Maggie L. Walker from Walland, Tennessee was enrolled in the Preparatory Department in 1902–03. She then taught school for two years, saved her money, and returned to the college in 1905 with the hope of encouraging her siblings—William, Rufus, and Julia—to enroll. In 1906, Rufus and Julia joined Maggie, and by 1907, William had arrived on campus. Excerpts from Margaret's letters tell the story of four mountain children who worked together to stay in school, care for their ailing parents, and help maintain the little family farm.

In July 1907, Maggie wrote to Margaret:

> I have been waiting to see if Rufus was going to be ready for school before writing you. He tells me he thinks he had better work and not go to school until after Christmas. He is working at Walland. He began the next day after he came home from school and has not lost a day since. . . . I have been working on my algebra trying to cover the work you will have this fall so as to be able to begin with my class in the winter but I have covered only about thirty pages and as my school began last Monday I will have little time for studying now.[23]

In March of the same year, Margaret had contacted Ella Bennett about a scholarship for Julia Walker:

> I do not forget the kind help given by your Missionary Society of the Williamson Presbyterian Church. I write now to ask that your Society aid in the education of a young girl by the name of Julia Walker. She was born in a mountain valley in East Tennessee. Her older sister had a year or two in college, taught short mountain school, saved her money and brought her brother and sister to college, trying hard to meet all their expenses. . . . Julia has a good mind and applies herself very well indeed. She will use her education to good advantage among her own people.[24]

In August 1907, Maggie asked Margaret to write to William, who was living in Lindale, Georgia. Margaret wrote,

> Your sister Maggie . . . is so deeply interested in Rufus and Julia getting a good education, that I [wish] . . . you could join them here. . . . I can arrange your tuition for you. It may be that you have been out of college for some time, but it will all come

back to you when you get started. You will probably be in my classes, and I will help you in every way possible. There are very few boys who have a sister as interested in them as Maggie has been in you and the other children.[25]

Like Maggie, Rufus felt a deep responsibility for his family and his community. In a letter to F. C. Gustetter, superintendent of the Westminster Church Sabbath School in Cincinnati, Ohio, Margaret described a very capable young man:

> Rufus is in college this year doing his very best work. He is so strong physically that no amount of exercise seems to weary him, and he has an equally strong mind, so that he is capable of very close application. He gets enough exercise by walking home on Friday afternoon after his college work is done, and working hard on the farm all day Saturday. He knows what it is to rise at the gray dawn and get the early dew of the fields and the first faint streaks of sunlight over the mountains, and to come in with the shadows of eventide to sleep the unbroken sleep of those who toil in the open. It is said that the world's hardest and best work is done by those who have had to hang on to the ragged edge of poverty. You may be sure that your student is none the worse for having to battle with poverty. . . . Rufus has one burning ambition to be a splendid teacher in his own rural community. He desires not only to impart instruction, but also to help in the building of character.[26]

A year later, Margaret gave Mr. Gustetter an update:

> [Y]our former scholarship student, Rufus Walker, taught a country school during the fall, but entered college again at the beginning of this winter term. He was able to save enough money from his salary to pay his own tuition, and has not asked for scholarship help this year. We admire his independence and respect him for his desire to meet his own expenses, leaving his

> scholarship for another student who needs it as much as he did before he taught school.[27]

Each summer, Margaret traveled to many remote mountain valleys to visit both the homes of her students and the settlement schools. To navigate the pass over Chilhowee Mountain into Happy Valley, located on the northwest fringe of the Great Smoky Mountains, Margaret rode a mule. Frequently, Wiley Boring from Happy Valley accompanied her. Wiley had entered the Preparatory Department in 1907 and eventually completed two years in the College Department. In a letter to Alice D. Winn of Woburn, Massachusetts, Margaret described Wiley:

> When I think of Wiley the first time I saw him in his own valley, and as I see him now, with neat collar and tie and polished shoes, sitting in his place in Chapel, . . . I feel that college has indeed done a great deal for him. He is a very bright boy. He was not in college the first part of this year because he dropped out to teach a school in a remote mountain valley. He taught in such a lonely little neighborhood that the children studied out loud and did not know any better. It was like the primitive days in the wilderness. I think he gained a great deal from teaching this short-school that will help him in college. . . . He thinks nothing of walking the thirteen miles home. . . . If he leaves here at three o'clock, he reaches home a short time after dark.[28]

Following his college days, Wiley remained in Happy Valley, became a leading citizen, and owned a store there for many years.

The Massachusetts State Federation of Women's Clubs established and maintained a settlement school in Happy Valley. Wiley, Mary (his sister), and other students from the valley received their preparation for college there. In the summer of 1910, Nellie Johnston, a junior in the College Department at Maryville, returned to teach once again in the settlement school short summer program to help meet her college expenses. Margaret wrote,

Wiley Boring

I went out to the closing exercises of her school and stopped for two days and a night in the teachers' cottage, where another one of our students was housekeeper, making a model home as an inspiration to the valley. Nellie had taught the children some flag drills and there were also interesting motion songs and some recitations. All the people came together in the schoolhouse, and after the school exercises we had a picnic dinner. It poured rain, but we were unconscious of the downpour, there was such sunshine and merriment within. The people had copied a good many recipes from the housekeeper and had prepared dishes like those they had learned from our workers. There were splendid layer-cakes, fresh bread and rolls, salad, preserves and jellies and everything that a heart could wish. After a long full day together, the people were still loath to go home when the twilight shadows fell.[29]

Nellie Johnston continued to take an interest in the children of Happy Valley. In a letter to William Darling of Summit, New Jersey, who had provided Mary Boring's scholarship, Margaret shared Nellie's plans for Christmas Eve:

> The valley people have never had a Christmas tree, and one of our college girls who was a teacher in the Settlement School last summer, is going back into the valley at the Christmas time to arrange a tree for the young people. Mary and her brother Wiley will be a great help in this work, as they have had the advantages of the outer world in their life here in Maryville College.[30]

A short time before Christmas, Margaret received boxes of Christmas gifts for the children of the mountains from the Circle of King's Daughters of Glen Ridge, New Jersey. Margaret repacked a box of presents for Nellie to place under the tree. Earlier in the month, Lena Aikin, who had worked with Nellie during the summer, had returned to the Valley with a box of gifts. This second box provided another gift for each child. In a letter of thanks, Margaret wrote,

> [Nellie] is overjoyed to be able to play Santa Claus in such a bountiful way. She came in with a wagon and team of mules to carry the goods out, and I have just bid her God-Speed over the rough journey mountainward, wishing her such a happy time at Christmas. She wished me to thank you for your generous share in making the Christmas entertainment possible.[31]

The workers in the Happy Valley Settlement School received an undreamt-of gift from Mrs. Eugene W. Chaffee of Moodus, Connecticut: a little organ. Margaret wrote,

> Your dear baby organ has been lying silent and well-behaved in my home awaiting the day when our two workers, Miss Nellie Johnston and Miss Nannie Maness, should take it up and carry it to Happy Valley. . . . [They] go Tuesday of next week. . . . The little organ will be part of their bag and baggage. If it had a voice

> with which to speak when it is set off the railroad train awaiting the ox-wagon to convey it to the teachers' cottage, what words of wonder you should hear with reference to the high mountains towering about it, the rush of the river close by, and all the wild notes of the forest, so unlike the stately, historical Boston from which it came. I expect to have a photographer go into the mountains this summer and take photographs of the children, the [schoolhouse], the teachers' cottage, and you shall have one of each that you may see and know, as far as a photograph can teach you, the new surroundings of your little organ. I do appreciate more than I can tell you your interest in this work.[32]

Mrs. Chaffee, a member of the Nathan Hale Memorial Chapter of the DAR, had a great interest in the people of the Southern Appalachians. A few years later, Margaret referred to the organ in another letter to her:

> The little organ which you gave has been such a help to the teachers, and the people of the valley have come to look upon it as their most precious possession. It has awakened a great desire in the hearts of some of the people to have an organ in their own homes and also one in the church, and one or two are dreaming of what it might be to have someone in the valley who could own an organ and know how to play.[33]

Margaret's missionary spirit was rekindled when she had the opportunity to work with students from other countries. Ludvik Burian from Martinice, Moravia, was one of nine international students enrolled in the fall of 1909. He received a scholarship from the First Presbyterian Church of Wilkinsburg, Pennsylvania. Margaret described Ludvik's life on campus and his plans for the future in a letter to L. R. Hagan, the pastor's assistant:

> Mr. Burian is one of the most brilliant students in college. He has acquired a splendid mastery of the English Language, and I believe is looking forward to work among the Moravians in this

Ludvik Burian

> country. He does everything in his power to help himself while here in college. He is the cartoonist for our "College Monthly," and his ready pen-and-ink sketches make him invaluable in arranging the bulletin-boards each week for the various social, literary and religious organizations of the College. Like his own people, he is deeply religious. The letter of commendation which he brought from his Moravian pastor to the President of Maryville College reads like one of the Epistles of Paul commending young Timothy to the loving care of the early church.[34]

In 1914, Ludvik earned a bachelor of arts degree. The last sentence of his biographical sketch in the 1914 *Chilhowean* expresses the admiration of the student body for his considerable talent: "All hail, then, to the genius of our class, King of College Spatter Club and Chilhowean artist, His Highness of the brush, Lord Ludvik Burian."[35]

Burian Cartoon

When ministerial students received help from the Presbyterian Board, they were no longer kept on the scholarship list at the college. In January 1911, Rev. S. J. McClenaghan, DD the pastor of First Presbyterian Church in Jamesburg, New Jersey, requested a ministerial student for the scholarship granted by his congregation. Margaret explained the problem and made the following suggestion:

> For this year at least I should like to have your scholarship aid Charles Damiano, a bright young Italian boy who has been sent to us from the Mission School at Middleton, West Virginia, which is under the care of Mrs. Marion J. Brooks. [Mrs. Brooks was a member of the Women's Board of Home Missions of the Presbyterian Church.] It was she who took Damiano from the gutter and set him on his feet, inspired him with a love of learning, led him to Christ, and pled for a scholarship for him here in Maryville College. When he came here two years ago he was not able to speak very good English, but he has mastered the language very rapidly and is one of the most brilliant and painstaking boys in his classes.

> I find it hard to interest organizations in our foreign students. Donors naturally think that the foreign born are inclined to be tricky and are not to be depended upon for any earnest work after their education is completed. We have had some rather sorrowful examples along this line. In sharp contrast to this somber picture, we have also had some very earnest foreign students who have not only served Maryville College while here, but also represented it in a most creditable way in their native lands. . . . I cannot find it in my heart to discriminate against these young people of less favored circumstances coming to us from alien shores. It would be sad indeed for Maryville College, which has sent out thirty-five missionaries into the foreign field in the last thirty years, to fail to consider it a golden opportunity for service in the training of foreign students who come knocking at our doors for Christian education. . . . I promise to be perfectly frank with you and if I see aught of change in him, will write you at once.
>
> Charles Damiano has the characteristic features and form, and perhaps temperament, of his people. He has the strength, and earnestness, and courage that has been acquired through the change in his ideals. He is not afraid of work, and all summer long he toils under ground in the mines of West Virginia saving his money for his expenses here in college.[36]

The year after Charles Damiano arrived on campus in 1909, Mrs. Brooks brought William Hughes to Maryville College. She asked the Sabbath school of the State Street Presbyterian Church of Albany, New York, under the leadership of Professor A. H. Mills, to provide a scholarship. Margaret wrote to Professor Mills:

> William Hughes . . . comes to us for the first time this fall. Indeed, Mrs. Brooks brought him to Maryville, helped to fit up his room, and has done all in her power to make him feel at home here before she leaves him to go back to her own work in West Virginia.

> Mrs. Brooks tells me that William's family live far up on the loneliest mountain trail, where I think there is no road leading to it, and look in what direction you will, there is never a house in sight or smoke curling up from any chimney. She also tells me that his father and brothers are among the desperate fighting class of the mountains. . . . In addition to the tragedy of this setting for his life, he lost a limb through a railroad accident, and has to go on crutches. Mrs. Brooks is arranging to buy an artificial limb for him so that he will be able to get around more easily. He is very sensitive about his trouble, and of course the shock of the terrible accident was hard on his nerves. I believe that he will find life in Maryville College the first real happy life that has ever been his. Mrs. Brooks is like a mother to him, and her love will follow him and her letters encourage him as the days go by.[37]

For Margaret, the hills and valleys of the Southern Mountains were filled with kith and kin galore. During visits in the summer months, she played with the children and encouraged them to attend the nearest short-term summer school. And when the time was right, she opened the doors of Maryville College to her young cousins. Margaret was particularly pleased when Lily and Cordelia Henry enrolled. The girls lived with their parents and five siblings in a one-room log cabin in Cosby, a valley that touches the eastern end of the Great Smoky Mountains.

Margaret wrote: "When Lily first came to college, she was so untutored to the ways of the world. She had never had a [toothbrush], or a comb and brush to call her own. She had never slept in a nightgown; she had never had a woolen dress; and she had never been out of her own little narrow valley."[38]

The sisters had no help from home in the way of clothing. Margaret described the father as a Rip Van Winkle who fished and rested the days away and the mother as a careless housekeeper. For Lily, Cordelia, and other students with similar needs, help came from many sources: boxes of donated clothing, small gifts of money to purchase essentials, and women from churches such as Fort Sanders Presbyterian in Knoxville who volunteered to sew for students who had not received training at home.

In the summer of 1912, Lily, a senior in the Preparatory Department, stayed in Maryville and worked for Margaret. Margaret wrote,

> We had many good long talks together, and I was able to see from Lily's standpoint just how the mountain people feel toward many things connected with a town or city. Lily says that she will always be glad that she has been able to get the double viewpoint. I believe that she will be a better worker among her own people on that account. . . . I paid her so much a week for helping me in the summer, and at the end of each week she laid aside one-tenth to give to the Lord. I ask what had first put it into her mind and heart to do this. She said that when she first came to our home years ago, she heard my mother say that she tithed, and though Lily did not have a penny then with which to tithe, she made up her mind that when she began to earn even a small amount she would give a tenth to the Lord. She told me of a temptation that came to her last year. By doing extra work for girls who were sick or absent from the dining room, she earned $3.50. She set aside 50 cents for the Lord and took the $3 to town to buy a pair of shoes. The ones she wanted cost $3.50, and she took her tithe money, added it to the $3, and bought them. After she had brought the shoes back to her own room, she felt so unhappy every time she looked at them that she asked permission to go back to the store and exchange them for the $3 pair. That was Saturday night. On Sunday she went to church and put the 50 cents in the collection. Monday, through the mail, she received from a most unexpected source a gift of a check for $3.50. She took the shoes, which she had not worn, back to the store and got the ones she wanted, feeling that the Lord had rewarded her making the sacrifice in tithing.[39]

Lily graduated from the College Department with a bachelor of arts degree on June 7, 1917, eleven months after Margaret's death.

Margaret was invited to speak at the general meeting of the Connecticut Daughters of the American Revolution on October 11, 1905. The invitation came from Sara T. Kinney, the state regent, who had learned of Margaret's work from Elizabeth Bullard, a former state vice regent. Following Margaret's address, "The Loyal Mountaineers of the South," the delegates voted to participate in the scholarship work at Maryville College. For the next eleven years, Margaret visited many DAR chapters throughout the state and made countless lifelong friends. Scholarships from Connecticut DAR chapters numbered more than twenty-five by 1910.

The Mary Floyd Tallmadge Chapter DAR of Litchfield, Connecticut, gave a $50 scholarship for Millie Hunter in 1910. When Millie arrived in Maryville from her home in Dorothy, West Virginia, Margaret described the fifteen-year-old as "rather small, with very dark hair and eyes, and a sweet face, although it was almost a week after she came before I saw it light with a smile. . . . I hope her life here will be so happy that sunniness will creep into her face and the shadows will disappear."[40]

By the end of the school year, Millie was thriving, and Margaret's report to Mrs. John L. Buel of the Mary Floyd Tallmadge Chapter was enthusiastic:

> She has been among those who made the highest grades in her class, and she is ambitious and anxious to come back and go on with her studies. . . . You will be glad to know that Millie is one of the best workers in the dining room of the Co-operative Club, faithful and ready, quick and most teachable if there is anything new to learn. She is kind and thankful and courteous with those who have to deal with her in this training. She is lovable in the classroom, and altogether she is a most promising girl.[41]

In another letter to Mrs. Buel, who was the Connecticut state regent and a close friend of Elizabeth Bullard, Margaret shared Millie's story:

> [Her] home is in Jarrold's Valley, among the mountains of West Virginia. One of the workers of that valley has recently been visiting here on College Hill, drawn here not only by her friendship for some of the teachers, but also by the five young people who have come from that valley to Maryville College. I have learned through her that Millie has a twin sister named Quinnie. When they were born [1895] and named, the father said, "Millie is mine," and the mother said, "Quinnie is mine," and since then each has clung to the child first chosen. The father's ideals and desires for an education for his children were higher than those of the mother, and as a result he was willing to give Millie up, much as he loved her, that she might go on with her studies here in Maryville College. The mother refused to give Quinnie up in the same way, but I have learned through Millie in the last few days that the mother will let Quinnie come next year. . . . The people of the mountains are so devoted to their children, that even to send them to a small place not many miles distant almost breaks their hearts.[42]

Elizabeth Bullard died in the summer before Quinnie enrolled at Maryville College on September 12, 1912. A short time later, Mrs. Buel sent $1,000 to the endowed scholarship fund. Quinnie Hunter was the first student to receive the Elizabeth Belcher Bullard Memorial Scholarship.

The years of travel in the Northeast blessed Margaret with the gift of many lifelong friends. Her letters tell of home-cooked dinners, invitations to attend concerts and visit historical sites, restful weekends in private homes, children, and family pets. In a letter of thanks written in May 1912, to Mr. and Mrs. Samuel McClung Lee, Margaret wrote,

> I cannot tell you how much I enjoyed the happy evening [in your home]. To one who is so constantly on the wing and

> boarding so much of the time, it seems lovely to come into a real home, with its pictures, music, flowers, and dainty meals. All these I found in your home, but the dearest thing I found there were those two blessed children, who gave me such a welcome and seemed glad to entertain me while the dinner was being looked after. It was a pleasant relaxation after heavy work to sit on the floor of the nursery and help the baby pile up blocks and tumble them over; to see Junior so careful that the baby did not get hold of a marble or a bit of paper, and open up his little heart to me about some of his pleasures and best times.[43]

In April of the same year, Margaret spent a week at Tucker Forge Farm in Monson, Massachusetts, as the guest of General and Mrs. S. Lockwood Brown. She shared two happy memories in a letter of thanks:

> It was a great pleasure for me to walk with you to the new farms where you are having such lovely homes made ready for the future friends who may come and make a new community of interest in and near Tucker Forge Farm. . . . It was so kind of you to make me your guest there all those days of rest, and I appreciate it more than I can tell you. . . . I fear at the eventide I shall always be longing for the heavenly music of your Victrola. I am hoping that we will have one for our College someday so that our students may have the benefit of the best music.[44]

In the early years of her scholarship work, Margaret formed a friendship with Mr. and Mrs. Charles Otis (current owner and son of the founder of the Otis Elevator Company) of Yonkers, New York. They provided a scholarship each year and welcomed Margaret, frequently, as a guest in their home. Mr. Otis wrote to Margaret in September 1907 to tell her about meeting former Maryville College student Charles Alexander: "[H]e is one of the most successful and enthusiastic evangelistic singers on the earth."[45]

In her response Margaret wrote,

> I am so glad that you enjoy the singing of our Maryville College representative, Charles Alexander. God is certainly using him in a most wonderful way in his service. He was in one of my college classes the first year I taught in college. He was very full of mischief, and there were times and seasons when I found it necessary to give him a recitation bench to himself. He always took it cheerfully when I called him forward.[46]

As each year on the wing came to a close, Margaret reflected on new friendships made and the renewal of old friendships. The letters she wrote to these friends revealed her warm outgoing personality. A few weeks before she left New York City in June 1916, Margaret wrote a note of thanks to each donor who had contributed to the scholarship fund at Maryville College. The letters expressed gratitude for gifts of $5 or $50, for a $100 donation toward the nurse's salary, and for three $1,000 contributions to the endowed scholarship fund. As she wrote each note, former students, such as Dora, Rufus, Mae, Hugh, and Quinnie, whose lives were changed by the generosity of others, came to mind. Margaret explained her gratefulness for each donation, large or small, this way: "It cannot be reckoned in mere dollars and cents, for when it builds into a life, it will become immortal."[47]

541 Lexington Ave., New York,
April 22, 1912.

Mrs. Norman B. Chapin,
Regent Torrington Chapter D.A.R.,
Torrington, Conn.

My dear Mrs. Chapin:

You may be sure that I have been on the wing speaking day after day at widely separated points, or you should sooner have had a letter from me.

You must know, even before I write you, how much I enjoyed my happy little visit in your home. I shall not forget that dainty luncheon which you had waiting for me when I came. It seemed good to come in the atmosphere of a home dining room again, with its array of old Colonial china. I enjoyed your pictures, too, because each seemed to have its own artistic value, and there is so much in the way pictures are hung, as to light and arrangement, to bring out their best points.

I am so happy to feel that your Chapter will have a share in the scholarship work of Maryville College. I am just getting ready to journey again, so cannot enter into details with reference to your scholarship student. The donor who has been educating my cousin Cordelia Henry died last October. I have not yet learned as to whether his widow will continue the scholarship in her husband's name. If she is not able to do so I should like very much to have her given to your Chapter. I will let you know about this

Thanking you again for the welcome which you gave me in your home and in your Chapter, I am

Sincerely yours,

Friends in the Northeast

Don't forgit thar's a whole day tomorrer that hain't bin teched yit.

—Margaret E. Henry

EPILOGUE

Yesterday, Today, Tomorrow

Both nineteen-year-old Nell Ross Kirkpatrick and her younger sister, Marivine, wanted a college education. In the late summer of 1907, Nell wrote to Margaret to ask if two scholarships were still available for the fall term. Indeed, no scholarships remained, but Margaret told Nell and Marivine to come. A few years later, Margaret explained to Mary Baker why she never turned away a student: "I can never make the students remain at home until I am fully assured that I have scholarships for them. This would mean the loss of a whole year out of their lives. I bid them come, and then it is for me to take up the field work and raise the scholarships necessary to carry on our work."[1]

The girls traveled to Maryville from their home in Mooresburg, Tennessee, a small, unincorporated community nestled between the Clinch and Holston Mountains in Hawkins County, and moved into Baldwin Hall on September 3. A short time later, Margaret contacted a friend, Mrs. George Jones of Melrose, Massachusetts, and asked her to consider giving a $50 scholarship to Nell, a promising student from upper East Tennessee.

Nell and Marivine Kirkpatrick arrived on campus with inadequate clothing and no money for incidentals. Nell was the eldest of several children, and her parents, who were in poor health and had very limited means, were unable to help. Both young women were in class five hours a day and had jobs in the dining room, which left little time for extra work.

Kirkpatrick

Margaret helped with small monetary gifts throughout the year and gave them clothing from boxes sent by various church groups.

Nell felt a great responsibility for Marivine and another sister, Lucy, who planned to enroll in 1909. To make college life easier for her sisters, Nell withdrew at the end of her first year and looked for employment as a teacher. For the next two and a half years, she taught in the rural schools of Hawkins County, helped care for her parents, and sent money and clothing to Marivine and Lucy.

Nell returned to Maryville College in the winter term of 1911. When the new Home Economics Department opened in the fall of 1913, she became an assistant in the elementary sewing class. Nell also participated in various activities on campus. She was a member and president of the Bainonian Literary Society and played on the varsity basketball team. During the summers, Margaret found work for Nell with the children and families in Happy Valley and Williams' Creek Valley (known locally

Cabin in Tabcat

as Tabcat). Nell worked diligently both in and out of the classroom and graduated with a bachelor of arts degree on June 4, 1914.

Following graduation, Nell taught for one year at Grove High School in Paris, Tennessee. Then, in 1915, she moved to Summersville, West Virginia, and taught home economics in Nicholas County High School. There, she met William D. Click, the vocational agriculture teacher and county agent. They were married on July 6, 1917. Nell and William had one daughter, Nell Jones (Nell Jo) Click. She was named for her mother and for Mrs. George Jones, who provided that first $50 scholarship in

1907. In 1930, the little family of three moved to Huntington, West Virginia, where William served as county agent and Nell was active in the First Presbyterian Church, American Association of University Women, the Women's Club, and Rotary Anns.

Over the years, Nell told her daughter about those early years at Maryville College and her deep gratitude for Margaret, Mrs. Jones, the professors, and the many work-study opportunities. When Nell Ross Kirkpatrick Click died on October 16, 1959, Nell Jo (then Mrs. Charles Marshall) sent a copy of her mother's obituary and wrote a note to President Ralph Waldo Lloyd: "Knowing what you and Maryville have always meant to my Mother, I knew she would want you to know."[2]

Nell's story was an inspiration to Nell Jones Marshall throughout her life. In 2014, a short time before her death, Nell Jo sent a gift to support two Maryville College students who were working during the school year and in the summer to meet basic expenses. One of those students was Loudine Louis. The gift enabled Loudine to attend her junior year without paying out of pocket. In an interview, Loudine said "I am still in awe that someone wanted to pay forward the gift that her mother received while she was a Maryville College student. I can't believe that the person who received the blessing was me. The gift means more than I can say in words, but what I can say is that I can't wait until I have the opportunity to pay forward this blessing from a stranger."[3]

Loudine, a theatre and psychology major from Lehigh Acres, Florida, graduated in the class of 2016. During the awards ceremony a few weeks before commencement, Loudine received the Bates Forensics Drama Award and was named the 2016 Outstanding Senior. Without a doubt, Margaret, Nell, and Nell Jo would have been pleased.

One hundred years later, Margaret Henry's legacy lives on

- through the endowed scholarship program (now the Maryville Fund), which was started by Margaret in 1907 and had a total of $13,250 by the time of her death in 1916;

Loudine Louis

- through the Margaret E. Henry Endowed Scholarship, which her friends established in 1906 and generously contribute to, after her death, as a way to continue her unselfish service to the students of Maryville College;
- through the few stories told in *Echoes from the Hilltop* and the many stories remaining in hundreds of her letters on file in the Maryville College History Room;
- through the work of the Maryville College staff, who strive to build a diverse student body, teach both in and outside the classroom, and believe in the value of the liberal arts; and
- through former students who remember the financial assistance they received and now want to pay it forward.

As Margaret herself wrote, "The success of Maryville College depends, more than her graduates think, upon their loyalty to their Alma Mater."[4]

Acknowledgments

When I was born on September 10, 1937, my father, James Alberto Cox, registered me for the Maryville College class of 1958. He was a poor, southern farm boy from Sharps Chapel in Union County, Tennessee. Born in the Philippines of a union between Daniel Boone Cox and Alberta de la Cruz in 1904, he came to the United States in 1914. Unhappy with only a sixth-grade education, he ran away from home to attend high school, supporting himself with odd jobs. James graduated from Maryville College in 1929 and moved to Philadelphia, Pennsylvania, a short time later. For over forty years, he was a cost accountant in that city.

In January 1956 I began my career at Maryville College as a biology major. Of greater importance, I met my charming mate, Rufus Bowers, a Southern boy from Greenback, Tennessee, who was commissioned as a second lieutenant in the Marine Corps at commencement in May 1960. His serving in the Marine Corps enabled us to travel extensively in the United States and Asia. Rufus has been a constant source of encouragement as I have worked on this book about Margaret Henry. His support of the project and his willingness to listen as I read aloud Margaret's letters have kept me going for ten years.

During Kin Takahashi Week (an annual gathering of alumni volunteers) in 2006, Dori May, the librarian who managed the History Room (archives) introduced Rosemary Potter, class of 1960, and me to Margaret's letters, which were being given only a cursory glance by two other volunteers who thought they were not worth keeping. When I read one out loud to Rosemary, we realized what a treasure of exquisite literature was in those musty old boxes from the basement of Anderson Hall. Dori May suggested that I work throughout the year in the History Room with other volunteers.

After Dori May retired, Martha Hess, class of 1967, a regular volunteer in the History Room, encouraged me in my quest to read all of Margaret's letters. During ensuing Kin Takahashi Weeks, many volunteers continued to read, sort, and organize the century-old letters. I am especially grateful to Elaine Boyer, Millie Sieber, Corita Swanson, and Montana Zerick, my grandson.

About the time my vision for compiling and publishing a book devoted to Margaret Henry for the Maryville College Bicentennial Celebration in 2019 became a real possibility, I had two strokes and was unable to continue working alone. Happily, family and friends stepped up and joined me in the completion of this project by helping in a myriad of ways: Elaine Boyer, Rufus Bowers, Julia Cooper, Elizabeth Evans, Dr. Gerald Gibson, Martha Hess, Chloe Kennedy, Robert Kennedy, Rosemary Potter, Sherilyn Smith, Corita Swanson, Dr. Ronald Wells, Mary Workman, Dr. Karl Yost, and Meelora Bowers Zerick.

I express my sincere thanks to these and many more individuals who assisted in making this historic book a reality. Most of all, thanks go to Martha Hess, who, as my ghost writer, wove Margaret's words into *Echoes from the Hilltop*.

APPENDIX ONE

Maryville College Buildings, 1868-1916

Margaret's letters reveal her pleasure in the development of the Maryville College physical plant during her years as scholarship secretary. This appendix lists the buildings and annexes constructed on the second site of the college from 1868 until Margaret's last year (1916).

Buildings	Year Built	Function
Residence	1868	Professor's home
Anderson Hall	1870	Instruction and administration
Baldwin Hall	1871	Dormitory for women
Memorial Hall	1871	Dormitory for men
Lamar Memorial Library	1888	Library
Willard Memorial	1890	President's Residence
Fayerweather Annex to Anderson Hall	1892	Instruction
Heating Plant	1893	Steam heat

Fayerweather Science Hall (burned in 1999 and rebuilt in 2001, named Fayerweather Hall)	1898	Instruction
Boardman Annex to Baldwin Hall	1898	Dining hall and dormitory
Bartlett Hall	1901	YMCA and gymnasium
Electric Light Plant	1901	Campus electricity
Second Annex to Baldwin Hall	1904	Dining hall and dormitory
Residence (1868) (burned-rebuilt)	1904	Professor's home
Elizabeth R. Voorhees Chapel	1906	Chapel and music
Ralph Max Lamar Memorial Hospital	1910	College infirmary
Pearsons Hall	1910	Dining hall and dormitory for women
Carnegie Hall	1910	Dormitory for men
Pearsons Hall, Third and Fourth Floors	1912	Dormitory for women
Fayerweather Science Hall, Third Floor	1913	Instruction
Swimming Pool	1915	Physical education
Carnegie Hall (burned-rebuilt)	1916	Dormitory for men

APPENDIX TWO

Magnolia Cemetery

The final resting places for Margaret Eliza Henry and several members of her family are located in Magnolia Cemetery, two blocks from the Maryville College campus. The corner plot contains the following tombstones and inscriptions:

James Gray Smith
[Margaret's grandfather]
Manchester, England
Oct. 1797
Maryville, Tenn.
Sept. 1875

[Author of *A Brief Historical, Statistical, and Descriptive Review of East Tennessee, United States of America: Developing Its Immense Agricultural, Mining, and Manufacturing Advantages with Remarks to Emigrants*, 1842]

Sarah Sayer Smith
[Margaret's grandmother]
London, England
Feb. 1806
Philadelphia, Penn.
April 1838

Eliza Smith Henry
[Margaret's mother]
Wife of
William Jasper Henry
Born in Philadelphia, Penn.
December 24, 1831
Died in Maryville, Tenn.
Oct. 7, 1909

William Jasper Henry
[Margaret's father]
Born at Henry's Bend Blount County
Dec. 25, 1832
Died at Camp Chase Ohio
Mar. 21, 1864
Confederate Prisoner of War
[Printed on the back of Eliza Smith Henry's tombstone]

Sarah Sayer Smith
[Margaret's aunt]
Born in Philadelphia, Penn.
May 1834
Died in Maryville, Tenn.
Nov. 1900

Jasper Henry
[Margaret's brother]
October 7, 1856–January 11, 1938
Born at Woodlawn
Blount County

John Smith Henry
[Margaret's brother]
August 24, 1862–July 30, 1942

Margaret Eliza Henry
Nov. 29, 1858
July 7, 1916
"Mizpah"

["Mizpah" is an emotional bond: "The Lord watch between me and thee, when we are absent one from another" (Gen. 31:49)]

"Oh promise me when I with bated breath
Will face the presence of the angel Death,
You will be near to guide my faltering feet
Whispering these words in accents low and sweet
Come to me sometime, from that distant shore
Caress and comfort as in days of yore
Triumphant over Death our love shall be.
Oh promise me! Oh promise me."
[Printed on the back of Margaret's tombstone]

APPENDIX THREE

Bettie Jane's Essay, Granny Stinnett's Funeral, Two Reports from the Field, and a Tribute

Found among Margaret's letters were a few essays written by her students and several reports from students and volunteers who worked during the summers in the mountain communities. A description of a funeral in Walker Valley and a testimonial written by a friend from Connecticut were also filed with her letters.

Bettie Jane's Essay

The following essay was written by Bettie Jane Henry from Cosby, who was enrolled at Maryville College in the Preparatory Department in 1911. She was a cousin of Margaret Henry.

> Christmas before I came to college
>
> As the Christmas season approaches I am reminded of the way we spent Christmas before I came to college.
>
> Our humble little home was situated in a very secluded spot in the mountains. The little log cabin was almost buried in the mountains and there was only one way out to the public highway

which could only be seen in one spot and that only in the winter time when the trees were not covered with foliage.

We were scarcely ever allowed to leave the hollow on Christmas time for the only way the men and boys had to celebrate Christmas was by shooting and drinking and our father said it was dangerous for children to be on the road.

We had very little for xmas. Mother saved the choice jellies and fruits to make pies. Generally our father brought one box of stick candy for a family of eight children, this was about the limit of our Christmas.

Although there were beautiful holly trees covered with berries quite in sight of our home we never tho't of a xmas. tree for we had scarcely ever heard of one, anyway what need had we for a tree there we[re] no presents to go on it.

We had heard of Santa Claus from other children of the cove, but if we mentioned it at home our father would say I don't want to hear any more such nonsense for there is not such a thing as Santa Claus.

If it chanced to snow we spent the day snowballing [and] coasting down the hill and often my older brother and I would go rabbit hunting and stay out most half a day at a time.

Once my father gave my two older sisters a doll, but I never had one until my sister returned from College and brought me one, she also brought an orange and a banana which were the first I had ever seen, yet in spite of all this xmas. meant a great deal to us as it does to all children in Christian lands. It was a holiday. It broke the mon[o]tony and we looked forward to it with great anticipation and pleasure.

Our mother is a devoted Christian and told us very simply the story of the Savior's birth.[1]

Granny Stinnett's Funeral

Belle Smith was an artist in Maryville. Her studio was on the edge of the Maryville College campus and just behind the home of her sister, Jane Bancroft Smith Alexander, who taught history and later English at the college. A few years after a short school was established in Walker Valley by the federated women's clubs, Belle accompanied the teachers into the valley one summer for the purpose of painting. While there, she became very interested in the work being done. As a result, when the summer term was over, she remained in the valley to work among the people. During that time, Granny Stinnett died. Belle was deeply moved by the mountain funeral and wrote a letter to Margaret. Granny Stinnett was the grandmother of Dora, Lillie, Millie, and Sallie Ann Stinnett.

Dear Miss Henry,

Some one must lend an ear that will patiently listen to these Valley tales; will you? Possibly Miss Clemens also, if you will kindly let her give a hearing. Nobody knows these people as you do, and you know I must talk to some one. The clouds are gathering black and thick-looking, and the thunder seems so close to us here. My boasted Sunday-school attendance of twenty-three was this morning reduced to five, a number sufficiently small to invite to eat apple-pie on the porch. (I trust these new features will not establish a bad precedent.) This poor attendance I do not take to indicate an entire cessation of interest; the threatening thunderstorm was partly responsible.

I am writing really to tell you of Granny Stinnett's death Wednesday last, of which you may have heard. She passed away very quietly in her sleep, evidently suffering but little. I went over with the Stinnett children Thursday morning early and stayed most of the day. We gathered flowers, hoping to make the room and casket a little more hopeful-looking, but I succeeded in putting only a spray of white flowers in Granny's poor hands.

Never did death seem so real and terrible a thing to me before; truly the poor see it in its repulsiveness as the wealthier never do. In that little room with its four beds about twenty-five people were gathered, while Mrs. Huskey and other neighbors were preparing the body for burial, bathing and dressing it—a day late—and closely watched by women and children. Four babies were being nursed in the room, one or two children a little advanced from babyhood were sound asleep on a neighboring bed; poor Grandpa Stinnett trying to sleep with his head tied up in a white cloth. All this going on in a dense cloud of smoke coming from coals under the bed, where I suppose disinfectant was burning.

Everyone was perfectly respectful, talking in whispers and deeply interested, but the ever-present curiosity repelled me at such a time. A whisper went around and the young people adjourned to the porch to see the bearers of the coffin wend their way up the hillside. It seemed as though Granny would have been pleased to see it, with the mahogany stain and its silver (?) handles. I did object to the paper inside! They put in a little pillow with a clean new slip, and Granny was dressed in a neat black shroud, black woolen slippers, and black gloves! Mrs. Huskey and another woman cut very neatly a "face cloth" about which they seemed much concerned, scalloping and notching the edges and cutting a little design in the corners. After all was done they stood about, evidently expecting to have no sort of service, waiting a few minutes only before going to the burial.

I was much concerned—it seemed so dreadful to bury the poor woman without so much as a prayer or hymn. Louie asked me to offer a prayer, and I most reluctantly consented, but rather than have none at all. While waiting, thirty of us or more, perhaps, gathered in that dirty room, sitting on beds or standing, looking into the empty casket, with the dead body on the bed back in the shadow, a queer little, doubled-up man started to sing a hymn, others joined in,—one of the dolefullest, most horrible of hymns about "hell's yawning below," and "eternal gloom," the like of which I never heard. This was sung with such a wavering and fluttering between notes, with quavers and semi-quavers, I caught but an occasional word. It was depressing enough, then the sobbing of both men and women and an occasional wail from a baby, made me feel that I ought to be in China. I could not keep still during the sustained and solemn silence that followed, and so spoke, spoke of what death should be to the Christian—the entering into a larger life, and how we should rejoice that this friend had gone on before us into a life of no pain or sorrow, a life of greater service and joy; how we should look forward to being with her, while doing our best to serve and help here, and not think so much of our own loss in this separation from her, [et cetera], closing with prayer. I said a little about Granny's kindness and about her life of service, and then we sang two verses of "Jesus, Lover of my Soul," the children joining in very sweetly. After-wards the body was lifted into the casket.

You may think this is easy for me—this work. I nearly died and groaned in spirit half the night at the things I said and the things left unsaid. I was never meant to speak in public. I only hope no one was offended because of it. The people gave their usual beautiful attention, and later the man of the dirge shook my hand, said he was proud to meet me and didn't know there was a woman like that in any of these parts! Just what he meant I couldn't tell, but think he took me for a missionary.

Later such a weeping and wailing began as I never heard, lasting until all were quite worn out, then the procession began to move down the hill, where the hand-car was used to carry the body to Townsend.[2]

Report from the Field—Walker Valley, circa 1907

Summer workers assigned to the various short schools in the mountain valleys of Tennessee and Western North Carolina sent reports to Margaret when the schools closed in late summer. She received the following report from a Maryville College student who worked in Walker Valley, circa 1907.

> I was trying to entertain a guest and get dinner at the same time. The woman was thin and worn with years of toil. She had walked four miles to Church that morning over one of the hardest trails I had seen in the mountains and now she was taking solid comfort in a rocking chair on the back porch, or summer kitchen as the mountain women for some reason call it.
>
> "Do you know" she said, as she watched me hurrying about, "I don't see how you stand it." "Stand what?" I asked, expecting to hear her speak of the loneliness of the place, or something of that kind. "Why, to stay here all summer in this nice house and have everything your own way and then have to leave it. I should think you would just keep studyen and studyen about it until you wouldn't be satisfied in Maryville."
>
> Summer before last a family moved into the Valley from North Carolina. To them it was like coming into civilization. They had been so far from neighbors and school that everything seemed new and strange to them. The children had never seen a flag and were amazed when we began to teach them to write as soon as they entered school. They attended our school regularly but would have nothing to do with our Sunday services and did not come to see us. When the summer's work closed I left sure that we had failed to reach them, but last summer the first time I visited the family, the woman took my hand in hers and said "Well you don't know how glad we are to have you in the Valley again and that the children can attend your school. They shan't miss a day if I can help it. It seemed so lonesome last fall when the

house was shut up. How good it will be to have it open again." I went away wondering, for they had seemed to care so little. But as the days passed and she remembered us with everything that grew in her garden, I began to feel her appreciation was genuine.

"I wish," she said one day, "you would tell us what vegetables you need that we have. Of course we don't want to send you things you have or don't care for, but we don't want you to go without one thing that we have and you need. It's little enough we can give but you are welcome to what we have." I did not like to at first but when they insisted I learned when they asked one to tell them frankly what we did not have and they provided accordingly. They were poor but we found that they took an honest pride in providing little things we needed. We were sent everything from bear meat to mountain ferns, but I threw away nothing except once an over-supply of beans.

We were very much encouraged in our school last summer. Before it has often seemed that the winter school did not leave the children any further along than they were at the close of the two months of summer school. But last summer it was all different. Hester Moore [daughter of Mary Ann Moore, second wife of Black Bill Walker] one of the [Walker Valley] girls who has been down here in Maryville College took up the work where we left it and we were surprised even after the long vacation to see how rapidly the children had advanced and how much they remembered. It seemed nice to think that [someone] from the valley had been able to do so much for the others.

One of the pleasantest features of our work has been the opportunity that it has afforded for the work among the Railroad people. Both years we have visited among them and received such a cordial welcome. Everything done for them is so much appreciated. Each year we have held one or two Sunday services among them. In this way we reached not only the families along the Railroad but also some of the men from the logging camp.

One day last summer a woman who lives beside the Railroad asked us to come and hold services at her home one Sabbath afternoon for those who could not walk far enough to attend our morning services. We told her we would come if she would let the people know. Sunday morning she asked her husband to fix seats for the meeting. He is not much interested in such things and refused, saying that no one would come. In fact he did not expect the preacher himself. That afternoon all the neighbors came, and a party of men from the camp and most of the people from the little settlement on Laurel Creek. It was interesting to watch that man construct seats while the crowd stood around and waited for them. However, he seemed pleased and afterward attended services in the Valley.

The people along the Railroad come and go, as a result no work among them can be permanent but we were glad to let fall a few seeds among them.[3]

Report from the Field—Sweetwater Valley, 1906

The following excerpts come from a report written by Flora Blanche Tullis, a member of a federated women's club, who taught for three months at the short school in Sweetwater Valley during the summer of 1906. The report was written on September 7, 1906.

When our school closed, on Thursday August the twenty-third, I felt that the summer had passed all too quickly and sincerely regretted the fact that such a delightful work must be relinquished.

The parting with our dear mountain friends was still harder to bear. It would be impossible for one to spend even such a short space of time among these people without forming a deep attachment for them.

It is not enough to give to the boys and girls that regular routine of school duties although this is likewise essential but there is a knowledge never learned of books. . . . One of the mothers expressed this same thought to us, in her own quaint way, it is true when she said "you teachers are different from the ones we have here; they can learn the children book learning all right but they don't teach them manners like you'se all do; we want our children to know manners."

As to the details of the work I will say that by the middle of July we had an enrollment of thirty-eight pupils making a gain of seventeen over the enrollment for the first day. . . . We were especially pleased with the way in which the interest and attendance of the boys kept up during the summer. Several of them were neither absent nor tardy a single day and many others who were compelled at times to work in the fields were genuinely grieved at the thought of the lessons they missed. . . . The girls were likewise faithful. . . . The girls were also very much interested in the cooking and sewing classes which were kept up regularly. This work appealed especially to the older girls, many of whom did some excellent [needlework]. While we have every reason to believe that a reform will be wrought in many a kitchen as a result of our practical work in the culinary line. In fact we saw evidence of this while we were still among them. We visited frequently among the people taking many meals with them and we found that a suggestion now and then as to the preparation of some new dish or a slight change in the preparation of an old one never went amiss. . . .

We made in all during the summer over ninety calls, and I will not attempt to say how many miles were traversed in that time. Suffice it to say that this labor, like all the rest, had its full compensation in the genuine hospitality of our mountain people. We can learn from them many lessons of unselfish and heartfelt kindness which is always extended to all who come beneath their roof. In summing up our summer's work I would say that after all, our labor was just the beginning of what may be accomplished another year. . . . My prayer is that this work may go on and on until there comes the period of full fruition, that there may be in Sweetwater Valley among the people we have learned to love the quickening of a new life as the result of the Federations summer schools.[4]

"Margaret Henry—Tribute of Love"

In 1941, Clemmie Henry (Margaret's successor as scholarship secretary) began making plans for a program to honor the memory of Margaret Henry. She contacted several of Margaret's friends and asked each to write a brief memory of Margaret. Mrs. John Laidlaw (Elizabeth) Buel (honorary vice president general, DAR, Litchfield, Connecticut) sent the following tribute in November 1941.

It was a great gratification to me to be asked to contribute to this program honoring the memory of Margaret Henry. Whatever I can say will be entirely inadequate, for what words can pay just tribute to such a rare and beautiful soul?

My memories of Margaret Henry are still vivid even after the passing of more than a quarter of a century. It was in the earliest years of the century that Miss Henry began telling the story of Maryville and her mountain people in Connecticut. As she pleaded for scholarships for her beloved Southern Mountaineers, she won the hearts of all by her rare spirituality and simple eloquence. Her hearers laughed and wept by turns over her vivid descriptions of her mountain people and their needs so closely were humor and pathos mingled in her stories. She opened a new field of endeavor for the Connecticut Daughters of the American Revolution. The chapters throughout the State gave scholarships and have kept on giving them year after year as a settled line of work.

A friend first spoke to Miss Henry of me when I was State Regent of the Connecticut D.A.R, but I do not remember how or when Miss Henry and I first came together. I had no sooner met her then I succumbed to the spell of her marvelous personality. From that time on she was an inspiring element in my life.

I have kept the letters she wrote me about scholarship girls for my D.A.R. chapter and for the Connecticut D.A.R.—letters in which the beauty of her spirit was so unconsciously revealed—in which her love of nature in all its mountain glory was expressed. This following quotation from one of her letters will explain what I mean better than any words of mine:

"Just before College opened I had a horseback trip to the top of Thunderhead, nearly 6000 feet high. From those lofty mountain slopes I caught such a vision of earthly beauty that Heaven itself seemed to come down and touch Earth, and all the cares, and sorrows, and disappointments of life seemed to melt away in the soft blue of the universe. But one cannot remain on the heights, in either a literal or figurative sense, for there is always the need of humanity in the valleys below where one's work lies."

"The need of humanity"—that was what inspired Margaret Henry in all her relationships with her college girls; she rejoiced in their success. Stalwart and sturdy as her own mountains, she told the story of her mountain people with all the masterful eloquence of a deeply sincere and religious nature. She well knew how to plead their cause—the cause of pure-bred Americans left stranded on their mountainsides by the march of civilization elsewhere. I can see her now, standing before my chapter assembled in my home and playing on our heartstrings as on a harp. Can we ever forget how she drawled out this saying so descriptive of her [easygoing] mountain people who refused in these words to be hurried: "Don't forgit thar's a whole day tomorrer that hain't bin teched yit."

Dear, priceless Margaret Henry! The very thought of her uplifts the soul to greater heights of endeavor—cheers the heart—purifies and consecrates one's life to the best that is in us to attain. I hold her memory in my heart of hearts thanking God that I was privileged to call her friend.[5]

APPENDIX FOUR

Donors

During the thirteen years Margaret traveled in the Northeast, she told the story of Maryville College to hundreds of organizations, churches, schools, and individuals. Significant help came from the Daughters of the American Revolution. Many of the chapters not only renewed their scholarships year after year during Margaret's tenure but also continued to support the work of the college in the Southern Mountains during Clemmie Henry's time as scholarship secretary. Here is a small sample of the various donors:

Churches

Acton Presbyterian Church, Acton, Indiana
Central Presbyterian Church, East Orange, New Jersey
Central Presbyterian Church, Erie, Pennsylvania
First Presbyterian Church, New York, New York
First Presbyterian Church, Stamford, Connecticut
First Presbyterian Church, Washington, DC
Oakland Methodist Church, Chicago, Illinois
Piedmont Congregational Church, Worcester, Massachusetts
Poplar Street Presbyterian Church, Cincinnati, Ohio

Clubs and Schools

Brighthelmstone Club, Brighton, Massachusetts
Coterie Club, Loveland, Ohio

Hawthorne Club, West Haven, Connecticut
Massachusetts State Federation of Women's Clubs
Pennsylvania State Federation of Women's Clubs
Pi Beta Phi Fraternity Club, Elizabeth, New Jersey
Smith College, Northampton, Massachusetts
Vassar College YWCA, Poughkeepsie, New York
"Young Men" of Cornwall Heights School, Cornwall-on-Hudson, New York

Daughters of the American Revolution and Children of the American Revolution

Abi Hamiston Chapter DAR, Plymouth, Connecticut
Amo Morris Society CAR, New Haven, Connecticut
Caroline Wheelock Society CAR, Danbury, Connecticut
Child of the American Revolution CAR, New Haven, Connecticut
Dorothy Ripley Chapter DAR, Southport, Connecticut
Emma Hart Willard Chapter DAR, Berlin, Connecticut
Eunice Dennie Burr Chapter DAR, Fairfield, Connecticut
Hannah Woodruff Chapter DAR, Southington, Connecticut
Katherine Gaylord Chapter DAR, Bristol, Connecticut
Lucretia Shaw Chapter DAR, New London, Connecticut
Mary Clap Wooster Chapter DAR, New Haven, Connecticut
Mary Floyd Tallmadge Chapter DAR, Litchfield, Connecticut
Mary Silliman Chapter DAR, Bridgeport, Connecticut
Mary Wooster Chapter DAR, Danbury, Connecticut
Nathan Hale Memorial Chapter, DAR, Moodus, Connecticut
Norwalk Chapter DAR, Norwalk, Connecticut
Ruth Wyllys Chapter DAR, Hartford Connecticut
Sabra Trumbull Chapter DAR, Rockville, Connecticut
Sarah Williams Danielson Chapter DAR, Danielson, Connecticut
Sibbil Dwight Kent Chapter DAR, Suffield, Connecticut
Sibbil Dwight Kent Chapter DAR, Windsor Locks, Connecticut
Stamford Chapter DAR, Stamford, Connecticut

Susan Carrington Clarke Chapter DAR, Meriden, Connecticut
Susan Carrington Clarke Chapter DAR, New Haven Connecticut
Torrington Chapter DAR, Torrington, Connecticut
Wadsworth Chapter DAR, Middletown, Connecticut
Washington Chapter DAR, Washington, Connecticut
Molly Pitcher Chapter DAR, Washington, DC
Chicago Chapter DAR, Chicago, Illinois
Boston Tea Party Chapter DAR, Boston, Massachusetts
Lexington Chapter DAR, West Stoughton, Massachusetts
Cayuga Chapter DAR, Ithaca, New York
Colonial Chapter DAR, New York, New York
Continental Chapter DAR, New York, New York
Irondequoit Chapter DAR, Rochester, New York
Oleans Chapter DAR, Oleans, New York
Chester County Chapter DAR, Philadelphia, Pennsylvania
Chester County Chapter DAR, West Chester, Pennsylvania
Germantown Chapter DAR, Philadelphia, Pennsylvania
Pittsburgh Chapter DAR, Pittsburgh, Pennsylvania
Phebe Green Ward Chapter DAR, Westerly, Rhode Island

Tennessee

Chilhowee Club, Maryville
Fort Sanders Presbyterian Church, Knoxville
New Providence Presbyterian Church, Maryville
Ossoli Circle, Knoxville
Second Presbyterian Church, Knoxville
State Congress of Mothers
State DAR Chapters of Tennessee
State Federation of Women's Clubs
Tennessee Christian Endeavor Union, Knoxville

APPENDIX FIVE

Biographical Sketch and Funeral Address

Margaret Henry died on July 7, 1916. Two days later her funeral was held at New Providence Presbyterian Church. The eulogist was Dr. Samuel Tyndale Wilson, president of Maryville College. His address was printed in a memorial booklet for her colleagues, students, and friends in Maryville and across the country.[1] Here are his words.

Biographical Sketch

> MARGARET ELIZA HENRY was the daughter of William Jasper Henry, Sr., and Mrs. Eliza Smith Henry. Her father was the son of John Henry and was reared on the John Henry or Davis farm, on Little River, at the mouth of Ellejoy Creek; and later on became a merchant near Ellejoy, and then on Main Street, in Maryville. In Maryville he was the partner of his father-in-law, Mr. Smith.
>
> Miss Henry's maternal grandfather, James Gray Smith, Esq., was born in Manchester, England, in 1797, and was married there, in Saint Mary's Church, to Miss Sarah [Sayer], in 1829. Their first child was born in England, but their second, Eliza, Miss Henry's mother, and their other three children were born in Philadelphia, Pennsylvania, to which place they had emigrated.

Later on the family removed, first to Jefferson County, and then to Blount County, Tennessee.

Thus it is seen that Miss Henry had mingled English and American blood in her veins.

Margaret Eliza Henry was born on November 29, 1858, at her parents' home on Little River, only two or three miles from the foot of the mountains which she always loved with such fervor and devotion. She was named for her paternal aunt, Margaret Henry, and her mother, Eliza Henry.

When she was only [five] years of age, she lost her father. He died a prisoner of war at Camp Chase, Ohio, and was buried there. He had enlisted in the Confederate Army early in the Civil War, and served in the First Tennessee Cavalry, Company K, under Captain William Wallace. While at home on a sick-leave furlough he was captured at his house in Maryville, the old Clute house, and, not long afterward, and just before the close of hostilities, he died in prison.

Margaret's mother was thus left a soldier's widow, with a young family of children dependent upon her. After the war her father and sister, Miss [Sarah] Sayer Smith, lived with her family, all keeping house together. There were five children in the family. Miss Margaret's death is the first to occur among these five children. Mrs. [Sarah] Henry Hood, widow of General Robert N. Hood, is living in Knoxville; William Jasper Henry, Jr., is a contractor and builder of Maryville; Gray Smith Henry lives in Oakland, California; and John Smith Henry is in the employ of the Southern Railway, with headquarters at Bristol.

Mrs. Henry was a noble and model mother, and while bearing untiringly the burden of the financial support of her children, concerned herself even more yet in training them for the filling of a useful and worthy place in life.

Her children attended the public and private schools of Maryville; and then four of them attended Maryville College.

For four years, Mrs. Henry had charge of the college boarding department, in order to help secure for her children the education that she coveted for them. Miss [Sarah] M. Henry, now Mrs. Hood, and Miss Margaret E. Henry both graduated from the College. They each spent five years in its halls.

The mother made the Henry home a place of books and culture. The children became great readers. Their grandfather, J. Gray Smith, was a very cultured man, of literary tastes. Mrs. Henry was a woman of rare strength and sweetness of character, and her children rise up to call her blessed. She had a mother's joy and pride in Margaret. She made her from infancy "a child of prayer"; and, moreover, was deeply impressed that she was also "a child of prophecy." The words of Margaret's birthday verse as found in Proverbs 31:29 seemed to her prophetic: "Many daughters have done virtuously, but thou excellest them all." She looked confidently for their fulfillment, and by self-denial and motherly guidance she did her utmost to bring them to pass. And when her daughter's life developed into one of such eminent usefulness and influence, she said, "I knew it," and was as proud and happy as a mother could be. Mrs. Henry died only seven years ago (1909).

Miss Henry became greatly interested in the first series of February Meetings, held under the leadership of Dr. Nathan Bachman, on College Hill, in 1877; and she then and there committed definitely and unreservedly her heart and her life to her Redeemer. She united with New Providence Church on February 24, 1877, a few days after her conversion, and has been during these years one of the most faithful and consistent and zealous of the members of the old church.

The first schools she taught were in Miller's Cove, in Blount County, and near Shannondale, in Knox County, and in Lexington, Mississippi, and at Rockford, in Blount County.

Through her maternal grandfather's family she was related to Robert Moffat, the missionary hero of South Africa, and for many years she has carried on a correspondence with Rev. John Moffat, the missionary son of Robert Moffat. But her missionary sympathies found deeper origin than genealogical relationships and family traditions; they found their abundant source in the personal Christian character, in her vital union with the Great Missionary, her Lord and Master. The missionary spirit of the College contributed also to the missionary motive in her life. She came to desire foreign service, and consecrated herself to it.

In 1882, the year when five Maryville students went abroad as foreign missionaries, she, with her friend and schoolmate, Miss Francina E. Porter, of Madisonville, went to Japan as a missionary of the Presbyterian Church. During the voyage, in a severe storm, she was injured in the spine by a fall. The injury was so serious in its effects that she was forced, much to her disappointment and sorrow, a year later, to return to the United States. Her injury for some time prevented her from engaging in any work, but after a year or so she began teaching again. For several years she taught in Maryville, and for one year in the Knoxville city schools. In 1890, because her work in Knoxville was too heavy a strain for her strength, she accepted, at a smaller salary, what surely could not have been much easier work—the duties of Matron of Baldwin Hall and Assistant Teacher in Maryville College. At the same time she was offered a position in Kentucky at a larger salary and with less work. What if she had accepted the easier position? Many hundreds of would-be students would never have reached college, and literally thousands of students would have had a harder struggle to remain in college. It was a momentous decision, and Providence opened before Miss Margaret a broader door than she had dreamed of, and sent to the College a gift of Providence whose name will be gratefully remembered so long as the College shall endure.

Miss Henry rendered three years' successful service as Matron, discharging at the same time and for one year longer the duties of instructor in English and German. From that time onward she served as instructor in preparatory English branches. She was one of the most conscientious of teachers, drilling her students into habits of accuracy and thoroughness. No teacher took a deeper personal interest in the students, and no one exerted a greater personal or more helpful influence upon them, and no one had a warmer and more loyal response from the students. Especially was her great influence manifest during the February Meetings, when, year after year, most of her students were won to the Christian life and service. Several strong men now in the Christian ministry were converted through her faithful efforts.

So enthusiastic a teacher was she that it was only with the greatest reluctance that she gave up even temporarily and in part the work of the [classroom], when her work as Secretary of Scholarships grew into a heavy burden; and the last catalog published is the first one in which she consented to have her name appear not in the list of teachers but in the list of officials of the College. She often spoke of the sacrifice it was to her to give up personal participation in the February Meetings and her daily contact with the [class work] of the students.

It was in 1902 that the president of the College, at the suggestion of Dean Waller, asked Miss Henry if she would be willing to make a trip in the interests of the scholarship and student-help fund that had been started on a small scale in the days of Kin Takahashi, that brilliant and public-spirited Japanese student of Maryville. She seemed frightened at the suggestion, and it was only when she was told that her friends believed that she could succeed in the proposed campaign that she was willing to give the matter any consideration. After considering it a year she came to feel that it might be her duty to make the effort; and when her mind was made up she bravely assumed the task from which her nature shrank so much. It required the highest moral courage for her to venture among strangers in the everywhere unwelcome task of seeking help from people already beleaguered by beggars. To fight on a battle field surely does not require any higher valor.

From the beginning of her work, however, she found friends. Rebuffs she had, but by far more sympathy, and, from the beginning, a remarkable degree of success. The first year she was in the field about three months, and during that time secured for her student-help fund $500.00 a month, or $1500.00 for the three months; and her traveling expenses were only $100.00. From that time to the present, the breadth and success of her work have steadily increased, until for years past she has been beyond question the most successful woman representative in such work that any college in the United States has had. This college year she was in the field eight months, and the receipts coming as a result of her work amounted to the remarkable total of $15,405.15.

From the beginning of her wonderful career as Scholarship Secretary, the Directors of the College have been filled with admiration and gratitude for the service she has been rendering. Year after year they have voted her hearty resolutions of thanks, and have tried to express to her their sense of appreciation of her self-sacrificing and heaven-favored work. And she has been as happy as she could be that God had given her this work to do. She said: "I had thought that God intended that I should give my life to Japan; but now I know that he had this other work for me to do for the Southern mountains and for mine own people."

And nothing could move her from the work. Her great eloquence and winning personality attracted attention everywhere. Two of the Boards of the Presbyterian Church made efforts—in one case, repeated efforts—to secure her as one of their field secretaries at a larger salary. A large school out West sought her services as their president. One of the principal publishing houses of New York repeatedly urged her to write a book, and were not satisfied with her refusal. But none of these things moved her even for a moment. Like Paul, she said: "this one thing I do." Her uniform answer was: "I haven't time or desire to make money for myself; what I want to do is to serve my dear old College and her boys and girls."

And how she did work and what success she had! She generally spoke once a day during the week, and several times on Sunday. Her itineraries led her through many states. Few lyceum lecturers have so strenuous a schedule. The DAR's [Daughters of the American Revolution] of numerous states, men's and women's and children's organizations both secular and religious, and a host of individuals, heard her with delight and aided her in her work.

Her marvelous success was due probably to four elements of strength: (1) To her genuine and transparent sincerity and tense earnestness. (2) To her unceasing prayerfulness and her absolute faith in God's leadership in even the details of her campaigns. (3) To her natural and heart-winning eloquence. Several leading men in New York and elsewhere told the speaker with much decision that she was the most winning and effective woman speaker they had ever heard. Her great-great grandfather was a brother of Patrick Henry, of Virginia. Her eloquence was certainly worthy even of this great Virginian. (4) To her remarkable social qualities. Every day she was the guest of some home, and so engaging and winning was her personality that her hosts became her warm and enduring friends, and for her they exerted their influence even year after year. Hundreds of these former hosts will sorrow deeply when they hear the tragic news of her departure.

When we attempt to appraise the great work she had done even as Scholarship Secretary, leaving out of account all the other conspicuous and far-reaching service rendered as one of the best of teachers and as one of the most active of philanthropic and church workers—a service in itself enough to make us pronounce her one of the very useful women of the generation—we feel entirely unable to make a proper appraisement of that work.

Certainly if we attempt an appraisement of her work from the standpoint of the money secured in response to her appeals, a wonderful fact presents itself for statement. It is that during the thirteen years she was Scholarship Secretary, she collected, not in pledges—for they are not here included—but in cash, for the use of the students of Maryville College the grand total of One Hundred and Twenty-two thousand Six Hundred and Ninety-two Dollars and Ninety-one Cents.

Of this great sum—several times the amount of the entire valuation of the ante-bellum college plant—$103,353.11 was contributed to current scholarships and self-help funds and has been used to help thousands of students; $13,250.00 was contributed to permanent scholarships and self-help work funds and will throughout the future produce an annual income of $795.00 to be used in student help; $2,698.80 was given for the salary of the college nurse; $1,636.00 was given as the beginning of a hospital endowment fund, to be used in the new department; $605.00 as a current agricultural department fund, to be used in the new department; while $1,150.00 was given for hospital and other equipment.

So much for the appraisement in dollars and cents of her toil of the past thirteen years. But what appraisements can we make of the good she did the students, the College, the country we live in, and the kingdom of Christ during these recent years?

While we despair of being able to make a correct or even approximate appraisement or estimate of this great good that she has done throughout this Southern Appalachian region, and throughout many States and even in the mission lands beyond the sea, we rejoice from the depths of our hearts that there is One that not only can make but has already made a perfect and exact appraisement of the good she has done and will do. God has it all written down in his book of remembrance, and has already uttered his approval of it as he has welcomed her home with the glad words: "Well done, thou good and faithful servant, enter thou into the joy of thy Lord!"

And in every part of Maryville and of Blount County, and in two-thirds of the counties of Tennessee, and in most of the States of the Union, and even in several foreign lands, are those who have been helped to a Christian education by this good woman whose servant body lies not in this casket. She gave her life in glad and willing service for her Lord and Master and for the young people of this section whom she wished to see equipped to serve efficiently that Lord and Master; and intense, indeed, must be her happiness as her Lord, pointing to the great multitude she has ministered unto, shall say—if he has not already said it—to her, "Inasmuch as ye have done it unto one of the least of these my brethren, ye have done it unto me."

Miss Henry died, at a hospital in Knoxville, on Friday forenoon, July 7, 1916. But Miss Henry's life work did not die on that Friday morning. It will go on forever, and will be a perpetual memorial of her.

During her lifetime, friends established and named funds in her honor, as a tribute to her. Several years ago, several friends united in contributing a fund of a thousand dollars to be known as the Margaret E. Henry Scholarship. A month ago, a good Pennsylvania Friend [Dr. Elizabeth Winter], who saw her off on the train for her last [homecoming], sent after her a check for a thousand dollars to establish another "Margaret E. Henry Scholarship." In the modest self-effacement that ever characterized her, Miss Henry, while deeply appreciating the generous love thus shown, would, if she could have controlled the matter, have had other names substituted for hers. "I do not want it to seem," said she, "that I am seeking honor for myself." A few days before her death, but when no one, as yet, suspected the approach of death, she was made very happy by the gracious act of a former pupil and [lifelong] friend of hers, who, while on a brief visit to her, subscribed and paid in a Margaret E. Henry Loan Fund of one thousand dollars as a tribute to her old teacher. No one could misunderstand such a gift.

These three "tribute" funds now become memorial funds; and doubtless many other Margaret E. Henry memorial funds will be established by friends who shall wish at once to honor her beloved memory and to perpetuate her work for the students of Maryville College; and these very appropriate memorials will help to make a reality what she often expressed as the fondest desire of her heart—that the College should secure so large a permanent endowment of work funds and scholarships, that it would be no longer necessary for any college representative to go out in search of current student-help funds. Of the $13,250.00 that she secured as permanent work and scholarship funds during the thirteen years of her service in the field, $4,000.00, or nearly one-third, came to hand, strange to say, during the last six weeks of her life; the gifts were two bequests of $1,000.00 each and two contributions by living donors, also of $1,000.00 each. Miss Henry was overjoyed and really excited by these gifts, coming in such quick succession; and she said: "I do believe that the tide has set in, and that we are going to receive a large number of permanent work funds and scholarships. Oh, how happy I am!" Very beautiful and useful will all these memorials be; but, after all, the greatest Margaret E. Henry memorials are: (1) the old College itself to whose welfare no one at any time in its history has rendered richer or more loving service, and to whose wonderful expansion of the past thirteen years no one has contributed more effectively and extensively; and (2) the lives of thousands of Maryville students that have been enriched by the education she made possible for them.

And these things we say about our Miss Margaret, as the inscription on the monument that New Providence Church erected to Dr. Anderson would phrase it, not because we fear that we shall forget her, but because we love to remember them as being true of her.

Funeral Address

It was a hot harvest day, a long time ago, on the sun-stricken plains of Esdraelon. The troubled prophet Elisha sent his servant to meet the Shunammite woman with the anxious inquiry, "Is it well with thee?" It was a time of death, but her reply, truer than at the time she thought, was, "It is well." On this day of harvest-home—on this day of death—we look at the placid form before us, and then at one another, and with tearful words we ask, "Is it well with thee?"

As to our dear "Miss Margaret," as according to our simple Southern custom we have called her, there is not a person in this great assembly whose heart does not instantly respond, "Certainly it is well, thrice well, with her."

It is well with her in that she has completed a great life-work. But was she not in the advancing flood-tide of her usefulness, and would she not have continued to render for many years an increasing service? So, indeed, it seems to us, as our broken hearts testify; and yet we know that she has, in spite of our thoughts of a premature and untimely death, completed a great life-work. Her life-story is one of a notable service nobly rounded out. Let no broken column be erected over her grave. Her life was a complete and symmetrical whole. It is well with her in this regard.

And it is well with her in that she realized her wish that she should "die in the harness." On a Saturday morning in March, 1913, Miss Henry telephoned to the speaker that she had just seen Dean Waller fall, as if fainting away, on the College Street bridge, and that she feared that he was seriously ill. A few hours later our beloved Dean had breathed his last. And Miss Henry sorrowed deeply, as did all of us, in the great loss the College had sustained. "But," said she, "what an ideal death to die! I hope that God will let me die in the harness." And God has granted her the desire of her heart; she did die in the harness. She worked up to the very end.

Miss Henry arrived at home on Saturday afternoon, four weeks ago yesterday. The next morning she appeared in her accustomed place at Sabbath School and taught her Philathea Class for the first time since she left in October, and, as it has proved, for the last time in her life. On Tuesday, in spite of illness, she visited her sister at her mountain settlement work, eight miles from Maryville, at the foot of Chilhowee Mountain. On Wednesday she consulted a specialist at Knoxville, and was ordered to bed. She returned home and obeyed the physician's orders. A week later she telephoned the speaker, reporting herself better and asking for a stenographer, saying that she had correspondence that could not be postponed until her secretary, Miss Gillingham, should return. For ten days she spent several hours a day in dictation, and arranged a considerable part of an itinerary for September, October, November, and December. Her friends had wished her to rest during the entire coming year, but she insisted that many new openings were too good to lose, and that she would take field work during the fall; after that she would rest. She also wrote many letters with her own hand, while lying in bed. She sent word by her stenographer that she was "earning her salt, even when in bed!" The letters she wrote during these last days were in her happiest vein, and surely no correspondent ever had a happier vein. She wrote letters of loving sympathy and, in cases that called for it, of earnest reproof to students who were the beneficiaries of scholarships.

She worked on Monday of last week, and would have worked on Tuesday had it not been the Fourth of July, and thus a holiday of the stenographer. On that evening she telephoned the speaker that she had decided to spend a week at a hospital in Knoxville in order to be under the observation of her specialist; and said that she was hungry to get back to her office on the old college hill, but would have to postpone that happiness for a few days. On Wednesday morning she dictated some instructions for Miss Gillingham, who was about to arrive, and wrote a letter to Treasurer Proffitt, enclosing the checks that had come to hand since her last letter to him; and then, at half past nine in the forenoon she went to Knoxville. That day she grew worse rapidly; the next day she consented to an operation, but horror-stricken friends were told that there was not more than one chance in ten thousand for her recovery. The operation was performed late on Thursday, and on Friday morning, July 7, at eleven o'clock, she passed quietly away, without having regained consciousness. Surely she had her wish; some of the letters she wrote had not reached their destination by the time that the voice that dictated them was stilled by death. She died in the harness; it is well with her in this regard.

It is well with her because she was entirely ready for her summons to depart. On Thursday afternoon they told her of the inevitable, and with calm resignation she said: "That is all right. I am in God's hands, I am ready to live and I am ready to die." Her last words were words of Christian confidence and love.

It is well with Miss Margaret, also, in the fact that she will be missed. There are not words in our language that are in the remotest degree adequate to express how sorely she will be missed. But is well with any one who has lived the kind of life that makes thousands miss the loving service rendered; and thousands will miss not merely her but also her service.

Again, it is well with her because her works will follow her. It is the glory of the sort of life that she devoted herself to that the life is immortal and the fruitage thereof amaranthine. In church work and school work we deal with immortal minds, and the impressions we make are as enduring as is immortality. While Miss Henry rests from her labors, those labors shall follow her throughout the Southern Appalachians and even to earth's remotest bounds. It is well with one to leave behind such an undying influence as is hers.

And then, too, it is well with her because not merely do her works follow her, but she herself is working on! Not toiling, for toil is earthy; but working, for work is heavenly. "My Father worketh hitherto and I work," said our Lord.

Certainly there is no doubt that it is well with our departed friend; she has completed a great life-work; she had her desire and died in the harness; she was ready to go; she lived such a life as to be terribly missed; her works will follow her; and new works will she do that are even greater than those great ones to which we do honor today.

It is well with her; but surely it is ill, pitifully ill, with us.

One of the greatest sorrows of our life has come to many of us—to her blood kindred, and to her heart kindred, for there are thousands that are heart kinfolk of hers, though unrelated by blood. Her kinsmen, her fifty colleagues of the college faculty, her intimate friends, her associates of the New Providence Presbyterian Church and Sabbath School and other organizations, and of the Chilhowee Club, and of the W. C. T. U. [Women's Christian Temperance Union], her townsmen and townswomen all, and her numberless circles of loving friends all over this land of ours—surely it is pitifully ill with us, for is not this lifeless body of hers on its way to Magnolia Cemetery? And shall we not soon hear the committal service recited over that body, and shall we not soon see these floral tributes kindly attempt to cover from our eyes her new-made grave?

Certainly it is ill with us, on account of the loneliness that will become the more intense as the realization of our loss shall grow upon us and as we shall no more meet her in the busy walks of life.

Allow me a personal word. Few will feel a keener and more painful sense of loss than will the speaker, who, for the past thirteen years has been sharing with Miss Henry the hard task of securing the help necessary to finance our rapidly growing College. Miss Henry's life and that of the speaker have been running strangely parallel courses. We were born the same year; we were fellow students at Maryville for five years; we were converted in the same February Meetings; we united with the church the same spring; we went out to the foreign mission field the same fall, she to Japan and the speaker to Mexico; a little later, on account of broken health, we returned to the home land the same year; and now for twenty-six years we have been serving together as members of the Maryville College faculty; while, to complete the coincidences, we have, as has just been said, been bearing together during the past thirteen years the heavy burden of securing funds for the expanding work of the College—Miss Henry working principally for current funds for the help of needy students, and the speaker working principally for funds for endowment, buildings, and equipment. Miss Henry's splendid success in raising up friends and in securing current self-help work funds and scholarships has had a large and decisive part in causing the phenomenal growth and remarkable prosperity of the College during these thirteen years.

The hardness of the task could not in any degree whatever impair her peerless loyalty to her "dear old Maryville." A secretary of a great church board had just heard Miss Henry speak; and very enthusiastic was he as he told the speaker that he had found in her one of the most eloquent lady speakers he had ever heard; and that he intended to secure her services for his board. The speaker smiled and replied:

"You are perfectly welcome to try; but I venture a prophecy that you'll never secure her services."

"Why not?" was the answer in a tone of surprise.

"For the good and sufficient reason that Miss Henry thinks that God called her to Maryville College and to its work, and she is supremely happy and satisfied in that service. The most tempting salary elsewhere would fail to interest her in the slightest degree."

And the prophecy was quickly fulfilled.

Is it strange, then, that it should seem to the speaker ill beyond all computation, so far as the College is concerned, that this loyal winner of great and perennial victories for Maryville should have been called away from the field of battle just when the Centennial Forward Movement was being initiated, and the need and the opportunity were greatest? Is it to be wondered at that, in the presence of this calamity, the heart is so heavy and benumbed that nothing less than the promises and commands of Almighty God could nerve one again for the battle?

It is ill, desperately ill, with us, and despair with regard to the future of the great work she has been doing would fain seize upon us. How can the College get along without her? A few months ago, we had our first great fire loss in a hundred years, when Carnegie Hall was burned to the ground. She sorrowed with us in this staggering loss; but kind friends are rebuilding the hall, and it will rise larger and better than ever. But the present loss is an irreparable one. Even God gives only one worker of a kind; he will not give another Miss Henry.

How will the hundreds of students who need scholarship help, and the opportunity to earn by work part of their college expenses, now be able to continue in College? Will the funds that Miss Henry has hitherto collected fail to come to the aid of these students, now that her eloquent voice is no longer raised in their behalf? If so, many eager students will lose their longed-for college education, and the world will lose the leadership these young people might have been trained to render. Heavy are the hearts of those who have served on the Scholarship Committee with Miss Henry, as they think of the problems that were so hard of solution even during her life, and that will now, with a rapidly growing college, and in her absence, be so much more difficult.

True, some one of Miss Henry's loving friends and kindred spirits in the faculty will, doubtless, enter the field to carry forward, as best she may, the work that must be done even when the worker has fallen by the way; and, doubtless, Miss Henry's friends will, even for her sake, graciously welcome the new representative of Maryville who shall take up the task that has just fallen out of these relaxed hands. But how ill it is with us that we must supply this unfillable place!

And how ill it is with the church of which she has been one of the most useful members, and with the community of which she has been called "the first lady"!

Yes, it is ill with us.

But, after all, it may be well even with us, if we but do the three things that we may be sure Miss Henry would enjoin upon us if she could speak to us from this narrow couch of hers.

(1) It will be well with us if we submit with Christian patience and resignation to the orderings of God's providence. She did thus submit, even with regard to this death that has befallen her; why should not we? Let us endeavor to say out of loyal hearts, "The Lord gave, the Lord hath taken away; blessed be the name of the Lord."

(2) It will be well with us if we find our courage centered in God's grace and not in human agents. She would say to us: "I have been merely God's agent; trust not in me, but in my great

Lord and Master. He has satisfied; he will satisfy you." Let us be brave in God.

(3) It will be well with us if we unite in doing our duty. Our ranks are broken; move up, and touch elbows; then forward march again! God will not fill her place, but he will carry forward his work, if we but fill our places; if all of us do our duty.

Less than a week ago, Miss Henry said in a letter that she dictated to a friend: "From my sleeping porch I can look out upon the blue mountains. Oh, how I love them!" Yes, she loved them, and their people; and now her God, who loves the mountains even more than did she, has translated her to a mansion whence she can look out upon the everlasting hills of heaven. She is still among the mountains—the mountains of God. And oh, how she loves them!

Notes

Foreword

1. Samuel Tyndale Wilson, "Biographical Sketch and Funeral Address" (speech, New Providence Presbyterian Church, Maryville, TN, July 9, 1916). The unpublished booklet is on file in the History Room, Fayerweather Hall, Maryville College Archives.

2. Rev. Robert Hugh Morris, letter to Dr. Samuel Tyndale Wilson, President, Maryville College, Maryville, TN, July 19, 1916. Rev. Morris was the pastor of the Central North Broad Street Presbyterian Church of Philadelphia.

Chapter One

1. Margaret Henry, letter to Mrs. John Parsons, New York, NY, October 21, 1909.

2. Chilhowee Mountain is a ridge thirty-five miles long on the edge of Great Smoky Mountains National Park. Little River cuts a wide gap in the middle of the mountain. The highest point on the eastern side is known as the Three Sisters (2,843 feet). The picture on the cover of this book was taken at daybreak from the Maryville College campus.

3. Robert M. McBride, introduction to *A Brief Historical, Statistical, and Descriptive Review of East Tennessee, United States of America: Developing Its Immense Agricultural, Mining, and Manufacturing Advantages with Remarks to Emigrants*, by J. Gray Smith (London: J. Leath, 1842; repr., Spartanburg, SC: Reprint Company, 1974). The reprint edition is on file in the History Room, Fayerweather Hall, Maryville College archives.

4. Samuel Tyndale Wilson, "Biographical Sketch and Funeral Address" (speech, New Providence Presbyterian Church, Maryville, TN, July 9, 1916). The unpublished booklet is on file in the History Room, Fayerweather Hall, Maryville College archives, and a transcript is included in appendix 5.

Chapter Two

1. Margaret Henry, letter to Mrs. Chauncy H. Marsh, Upper Montclair, NJ, October 9, 1914.

2. Margaret Henry, written account of her trip to the top of Thunderhead Mountain in August 1912, n.d.

3. Margaret Henry, letter to Mrs. Annie Russell Marble, Worcester, MA, July 5, 1911.

4. Margaret Henry, letter to Mrs. George E. Scott, Philadelphia, PA, November 16, 1910.

5. Margaret Henry, letter to Mrs. Carl Viets, Lucretia Shaw Chapter, DAR, New London, CT, December 15, 1909.

6. Margaret Henry, letter to Mrs. H. G. MacDonald, Wilkinsburg, PA, January 28, 1914.

7. Margaret Henry, letter to Miss Anne Waite, Secretary, the Cheerful Workers Circle of the King's Daughters, Greenwich Presbyterian Church, New York, NY, November 7, 1913.

8. Margaret Henry, letter to Miss Bertha Douglas, Aspinwall, PA, November 20, 1914.

9. Margaret Henry, letter to Miss Harriette Campfield, East Orange, NJ, November 13, 1912.

10. Margaret Henry, letter to Miss Edith H. Fairfield, Good Cheer Club, East Orange, NJ, April 17, 1913.

11. Margaret Henry, letter to Master Paul Black, Wilkinsburg, PA, January 1, 1914.

12. Margaret Henry, letter to Mr. and Mrs. Walter S. Lewis, St. Paul Presbyterian Church, Philadelphia, PA, June 3, 1910.

13. Margaret Henry, letter to Mrs. Robert H. Cushman, Sunday School Class of Boys, Monson, MA, January 3, 1912.

14. Margaret Henry, letter to Mrs. Lewis E. Tracy, Thursday Morning Fort Nightly Club, Dorchester, MA, November 7, 1912.

15. Margaret Henry, letter to Mr. and Mrs. J. R. Collingwood, Princeton Presbyterian Church, Philadelphia, PA, December 20, 1910.

16. Margaret Henry, letter to Mrs. Percy Wightman, University Heights, NY, September 7, 1907.

17. Margaret Henry, letter to Miss Gladys Stephenson, Bradford Academy, Bradford, MA, April 16, 1913.

18. Margaret Henry, letter to Miss Susan Howell, Class 31 of Memorial Presbyterian Church, Rochester, NY, November 29, 1912.

19. Margaret Henry, letter to Miss Susan Howell, Class 31 of Memorial Presbyterian Church, Rochester, NY, January 13, 1913.

20. Margaret Henry, letter to Miss Susan Howell, Class 31 of Memorial Presbyterian Church, Rochester, NY, September 17, 1913.

21. Margaret Henry, letter to Miss Eleanor G. Parks, East Allegheny, PA, October 3, 1912.

22. Margaret Henry, letter to Mr. H. Frank Pierson, Orange, NJ, September 21, 1910.

23. Margaret Henry, letter to Mrs. A. Romeyn Pierson, Glen Ridge, NJ, January 20, 1911.

24. Margaret Henry, letter to Mrs. J. R. Woodhull, Regent, Mary Silliman Chapter, DAR, Bridgeport, CT, November 2, 1910.

25. Margaret Henry, letter to Mrs. H. T. Porter, Philadelphia, PA, December 26, 1911.

26. Margaret Henry, letter to Mrs. H. Carpenter, Wilkinsburg, PA, February 10, 1915.

27. Margaret Henry, letter to Mrs. M. E. Walling, Victor, NY, December 19, 1906.

28. Margaret Henry, letter to H. C. Gara, Esq., Superintendent; William E. Bradley, Esq.; and Mr. and Mrs. Collingwood, Princeton Sunday School, Philadelphia, PA, December 13, 1910.

29. Margaret Henry, letter to Miss Edna Woodruff, Southington, CT, May 7, 1913.

30. Margaret Henry, letter to Mrs. Sara E. Peirce, President, Dorchester Daughters of Maine, Dorchester, MA, October 8, 1912.

31. Margaret Henry, letter to Mrs. Edward Croft, Lockport, NY, November 16, 1908.

32. Margaret Henry, letter to Mrs. Frank Hartwell, Danbury, CT, May 10, 1913.

Chapter Three

1. Margaret Henry, letter to Miss Ida M. Tracy, Thursday Morning Fortnightly Club, Dorchester Center, MA, August 19, 1913.

2. Margaret Henry, letter to Dr. Samuel Tyndale Wilson, President, Maryville College, Maryville, TN, June 6, 1910.

3. Margaret Henry, letter to Mr. and Mrs. S. Edgar Briggs, East Orange, NJ, December 10, 1910.

4. Margaret Henry, letter to Miss Bertha Reed, Memorial Church, Springfield, MA, May 17, 1911.

5. Dr. Samuel Tyndale Wilson, letter to Miss Margaret E. Henry, Franklin Square House, Boston, MA, March 8, 1912.

6. Dr. Samuel Tyndale Wilson, letter to Miss Margaret E. Henry, Franklin Square House, Boston, MA, March 8, 1912.

7. Margaret Henry, letter to Miss Molly Caldwell, Matron, Baldwin Hall, Maryville College, Maryville, TN, March 15, 1912.

8. Margaret Henry, letter to Dr. Samuel Tyndale Wilson, President, Maryville College, Maryville, TN, December 29, 1911.

9. *Annual Report for 1907–08 of the President and Faculty of Maryville College*, May 26, 1908 (unpublished record book for May 1902–June 1913), 2. The record book is on file in the History Room, Fayerweather Hall, Maryville College archives.

10. Ben Cunningham, "Minutes of the Board of Directors," May 26, 1908 (unpublished record book, Maryville College, Maryville, TN, May

27, 1891–January 10, 1912), 262. The record book is on file in the History Room, Fayerweather Hall, Maryville College archives.

11. Margaret Henry, letter to Major Ben Cunningham, Treasurer, Maryville College, Maryville, TN, January 25, 1909.

12. Margaret Henry, letter to Miss Annie D. Robinson, Shadyside Presbyterian Church, Pittsburgh, PA, January 13, 1913.

13. Margaret Henry, letter to Mrs. Alexander Peacock, Shadyside Presbyterian Church, Pittsburgh, PA, March 31, 1915.

14. Margaret Henry, letter to Mrs. H. H. Wagner, East Orange, NJ, January 12, 1915.

15. Margaret Henry, letter to Dr. Samuel Tyndale Wilson, President, Maryville College, Maryville, TN, May 10, 1912.

16. Alice A. Gillingham, letter to Professor Clinton Gillingham, Maryville College, Maryville, TN, May 27, 1912. Professor Gillingham was professor of the English Bible, head of the Bible Training Department, and registrar.

17. Margaret Henry, letter to Mrs. Arthur P. Felton, Central Congregational Church, West Newton, MA, November 21, 1906.

18. Margaret Henry, letter to Mrs. James Flint, Weymouth, MA, September 12, 1912.

19. Alice A. Gillingham, letter written for Margaret Henry to Rev. John Allison, DD, Point Breeze Presbyterian Church, Pittsburgh, PA, January 9, 1913.

20. Margaret Henry, letter to Mrs. Catherine C. Trent, New Haven, CT, October 18, 1910.

21. Margaret Henry, letter to Mrs. F. W. Goddard, President of the National Society Colonial Dames, Colorado Springs, CO, November 9, 1912.

22. Margaret Henry, letter to Miss Elizabeth Patten, Home Department, Middletown, CT, April 18, 1916.

23. Margaret Henry, letter to Dr. Albert P. Mills, Sunday School of the State Street Presbyterian Church, Albany, NY, December 2, 1914.

24. *Maryville College Bulletin* 10, no. 1 (May 1911), 27.

25. Margaret Henry, letter to Miss Helen. J. Sanborn, Winter Hill Station, Boston, MA, November 24, 1913.

26. Margaret Henry, letter to Mrs. Jasper Corning, Rye, NY, November 28, 1910.

27. Margaret Henry, letter to Miss Ruth D. Yeatman, Treasurer, New Century Club, Kennett Square, PA, May 24, 1916.

28. Margaret Henry, letter to Mrs. George Scott, Regent, Chester County Chapter, DAR, Philadelphia, PA, October 13, 1914.

29. Margaret Henry, letter to Mrs. T. H. Foulds, Glens Falls, NY, October 14, 1912.

30. *Maryville College Bulletin* 11, no. 1 (May 1912), 26.

31. Margaret Henry, letter to Miss Alice Clemens, teacher, Preparatory Department, Maryville College, Maryville, TN, March 26, 1912.

32. Margaret Henry, letter to Mrs. W. K. Porter, Secretary, New England Women's Club, Boston, MA, January 15, 1912.

33. "Program of the Ninetieth Annual Commencement of Maryville College" (program, Maryville College, Maryville, TN, May 28–June 2, 1909). The program is on file in the History Room, Fayerweather Hall, Maryville College archives.

34. Margaret Henry, letter to Mrs. Edward Sudbury, Mount Vernon, NY, June 5, 1909.

35. Margaret Henry, letter to Mrs. Peter Mason Bartlett, Maryville, TN, November, 12, 1908.

36. Helen, Wallace, Andrus, Gretchen, and Edward Snyder. Letter to Rev. William Thaw Bartlett, Katonah Presbyterian Church, Katonah, NY, November 8, 1908.

37. Margaret Henry, letter to Mrs. Edna C. Bowker, Morning Club, Brookline, MA, December 8, 1906.

38 Margaret Henry, letter to Miss Sarah E. Lamb, Pleasantville, PA, December 8, 1906.

39. Margaret Henry, letter to Mrs. R. D. Dudley, Rockland, MA, October 1, 1913.

40. Margaret Henry, letter to Mrs. Harold Pierce, Missionary Society of the Bryn Mawr Presbyterian Church, Haverford, PA, January 28, 1907.

41. James A. Burnett, letter to Dr. Samuel Tyndale Wilson, President, Maryville College, Maryville, TN, May 12, 1915.

42. Margaret Henry, letter to Mrs. J. W. Reisner, Washington, DC, October 14, 1912.

43. Margaret Henry, letter to Mrs. C. W. Hinckley, Missionary Society, Kenwood Evangelical Church, Chicago, IL, November 13, 1907.

44. Margaret Henry, letter to Mrs. Frank Lebar, Overbrook, PA, May 30, 1916.

45. Margaret Henry, letter to Mr. F. C. Gustetter, Superintendent, Westminster Sabbath School, Cincinnati, OH, April 19, 1913.

46. Margaret Henry, letter to Miss Mary W. Knapp, Washington, DC, September 19, 1912.

47. Margaret Henry, letter to Mr. John Elliott, Oswego College, Oswego, KS, March 25, 1913.

Chapter Four

1. Mrs. Charles A. Perkins, letter of introduction for Margaret E. Henry, Maryville College, Maryville, TN, January 16, 1906. Mrs. Perkins, of Knoxville, TN, was a member of Ossoli Circle, the first federated women's club in the South, and the board of directors of the General Federation of Women's Clubs.

2. Margaret Henry, letter to Mrs. Frederick A. Strong, Federated Women's Club of Bridgeport, CT, April 25, 1907.

3. Margaret Henry, letter to Mrs. William W. Crossly, New York, NY, January 17, 1912.

4. Rev. Robert Hugh Morris, letter to Dr. Samuel Tyndale Wilson, President, Maryville College, Maryville, TN, July 19, 1916. Rev. Morris was the pastor of the Central North Broad Street Presbyterian Church, Philadelphia, PA.

5. Margaret Henry, letter to Rev. William Wright Stoddart, DD, Hill Memorial Presbyterian Church, Rochester, NY, March 12, 1912.

6. Margaret Henry, letter to Mrs. Sidney McDougall and Mrs. Fredric W. Danforth, Women's Guild of the North Presbyterian Church, Buffalo, NY, February 24, 1915.

7. Margaret Henry, letter to Miss Clara Quinby, Newark, NJ, November 19, 1909.

8. Margaret Henry, letter to Mrs. H. T. Porter, Philadelphia, PA, December 26, 1911.

9. Margaret Henry, letter to Mr. and Mrs. John B. Ramsey, Baltimore, MD, April 4, 1913.

10. Margaret Henry, letter to Mr. J. W. Topley, Superintendent, North Congregational Church Sunday School, Haverhill, MA, December 15, 1915.

11. Margaret Henry, letter to Mrs. Maude Battelle Warren, Dorchester, MA, November 13, 1914.

12. Margaret Henry, letter to Mrs. F. W. Brode, Memphis, TN, November 17, 1909.

13. Margaret Henry, letter to Dr. and Mrs. J. T. Kerr, Elizabeth, NJ, November 3, 1910.

14. Margaret Henry, letter to Miss Mae Swanner, Meadow, TN, September 10, 1907.

15. Margaret Henry, letter to Mrs. G. H. Noxon, Regent, Norwalk Chapter, DAR, Darien, CT, December 6, 1912.

16. Margaret Henry, letter to Mrs. G. H. Noxon, Norwalk Chapter, DAR, Darien, CT, December 21, 1910.

17. Margaret Henry, letter to Mrs. F. P. Hotchkiss, Niagara Falls, NY, July 20, 1911.

18. Margaret Henry, letter to Miss Harriette S. Campfield, East Orange, NJ, December 10, 1910.

19. Margaret Henry, letter to Miss Grace Cleveland Porter, Summit, NJ, September 27, 1910.

20. Margaret Henry, letter to Miss Grace Cleveland Porter, Summit, NJ, March 13, 1911.

21. Margaret Henry, letter to Mrs. F. W. Brode, Memphis, TN, December 6, 1909.

22. Margaret Henry, letter to Miss Ethel Patterson, Treasurer, Young People's Association, Orange, NJ, March 15, 1911.

23. Maggie Walker, letter to Miss Margaret E. Henry, Maryville College, Maryville, TN, July 27, 1907.

24. Margaret Henry, letter to Miss Ella Bennett, Missionary Society, Williamson Presbyterian Church, Williamson, NY, March 18, 1907.

25. Margaret Henry, Letter to Mr. William Walker, Lindale, GA, August 17, 1907.

26. Margaret Henry, letter to Mr. F. C. Gustetter, Superintendent, Westminster Church Sabbath School, Cincinnati, OH, March 6, 1912.

27. Margaret Henry, letter to Mr. F. C. Gustetter, Superintendent, Westminster Church Sabbath School, Cincinnati, OH, January 14, 1913.

28. Margaret Henry, letter to Mrs. Alice D. Winn, President, Woburn Women's Club, Woburn, MA, January 14, 1910.

29. Margaret Henry, letter to Mrs. Maria D. Whicher, Dorchester, MA, October 11, 1910.

30. Margaret Henry, letter to William Darling, Esq., Summit, NJ, December 10, 1910.

31. Margaret Henry, letter to Mrs. F. B. Moore, Corresponding Secretary, Circle of King's Daughters, Glen Ridge, NJ, December 21, 1910.

32. Margaret Henry, letter to Mrs. Eugene Chaffee, Nathan Hale Memorial Chapter, DAR, Moodus, CT, May 28, 1908.

33. Margaret Henry, letter to Mrs. Eugene Chaffee, Nathan Hale Memorial Chapter, DAR, Moodus, CT, September 19, 1910.

34. Margaret Henry, letter to Mr. L. R. Hagan, Assistant to the Pastor, First Presbyterian Church, Wilkinsburg, PA, April 10, 1913.

35. *Chilhowean* '14 (annual college publication, Columbus, OH: Champlin Press, 1914), 26. *Chilhowean* '14 is on file in the History Room, Fayerweather Hall, Maryville College archives.

36. Margaret Henry, letter to Rev. S. J. McClenaghan, DD, First Presbyterian Church, Jamesburg, NJ, January 27, 1911.

37. Margaret Henry, letter to Professor A. H. Mills, State Street Presbyterian Church, Albany, NY, October 5, 1910.

38. Margaret Henry, letter to Mrs. F. H. Bassett, Bridgeport, CT, November 11, 1910.

39. Margaret Henry, letter to Mrs. Linnie G. Finney, Washington, DC, November 11, 1912.

40. Margaret Henry, letter to Mrs. John L. Buel, Mary Floyd Tallmadge Chapter, DAR, Litchfield, CT, October 6, 1910.

41. Margaret Henry, letter to Mrs. John L. Buel, Mary Floyd Tallmadge Chapter, DAR, Litchfield, CT, June 30, 1911.

42. Margaret Henry, letter to Mrs. John Laidlow Buel, Regent, Connecticut State DAR, East Meadows, Litchfield, CT, March 7, 1911.

43. Margaret Henry, letter to Mr. and Mrs. Samuel McClung Lee, Ben Avon, PA, May 9, 1912.

44. Margaret Henry, letter to General and Mrs. S. Lockwood Brown, Tucker Forge Farm, Monson, MA, April 17, 1912.

45. Charles R. Otis, letter to Miss Margaret Henry, Maryville College, Maryville, TN, September 27, 1907.

46. Margaret Henry, letter to Mr. Charles R. Otis, Yonkers, NY, October 1, 1907.

47. Margaret Henry, letter to Mrs. Albert Winslow Nickerson, Dedham, MA, March 5, 1912.

Epilogue

1. Margaret Henry, letter to Miss Mary E. Baker, Newark, NJ, January 6, 1912.

2. Nell Jones Click Marshall, letter to Dr. Ralph Waldo Lloyd, President, Maryville College, Maryville, TN, October 24, 1959.

3. *Focus* 3, no. 1 (Spring 2015), 18. Issues of *Focus* are on file in the History Room, Fayerweather Hall, Maryville College archives.

4. Margaret Henry, letter to Rev. John G. Newman, DD, Wyoming, OH, January 29, 1907.

Appendix Three

1. Bettie Jane Henry, "Christmas before I Came to College" (essay, Maryville College, circa 1911).

2. Belle Smith, letter to Margaret Henry, Maryville College, Maryville, TN, 1907.

3. "Report from the Field—Walker Valley," report to Margaret Henry, Maryville College, Maryville, TN, circa 1907.

4. Flora Blanche Tullis, "Report from the Field—Sweetwater Valley," report to Margaret Henry, Maryville College, Maryville, TN, September 7, 1906.

5. Mrs. John Laidlaw (Elizabeth) Buel, "Margaret Henry—Tribute of Love," message to Clemmie Henry, Maryville College, Maryville, TN, November 1941.

Appendix Five

1. Samuel Tyndale Wilson, "Biographical Sketch and Funeral Address" (speech, New Providence Presbyterian Church, Maryville, TN, July 9, 1916). The unpublished booklet is on file in the History Room, Fayerweather Hall, Maryville College Archives.

Index

A
Agriculture Department (Maryville College), 56–57
Aikin, Lena, 94
Alexander, Charles, 103–104
Alexander, Jane Bancroft Smith, 123
Anderson, Isaac, 50
Anderson, John, 51
Anderson Hall, ix, 41
Angier, Albert E., 43
Angier Self-help Work and Loan Fund, 43

B
Bachman, Nathan, 5
Bainonian Literary Society, 108
Baldwin Hall, 6, 36–37
Barnes, Jasper, 58
Bartlett, Alexander, 61
Bartlett, Cora, 5–6
Bartlett, Peter Mason, 1, 60–61
Bartlett, William Thaw, 61
Bartlett Hall, 55*f*
Bennett, Ella, 90
Bible Training Department (Maryville College), 56
Black, Paul, 24
Boring, Wiley, 92, 93*f*
Bowker, Edna, 62
Bradford Academy, 27–28
Brief Historical, Statistical, and Descriptive Review of East Tennessee, United States of America, A (Smith), 2–3
Brode, Mrs. F. W., 84
Brooks, Mrs. Marion J., 97
Brown, Ernest Chalmers, 64*f*, 65
Brown, Gen. and Mrs. S. Lockwood, 103
Bryn Mawr Presbyterian Church of Haverford, 63
Buchanan, Grace, 22
Buel, Elizabeth, 130–131
Buel, John L., 101–102
Bullard, Elizabeth, 101–102
Burian, Ludvik, 95–96, 96*f*, 97*f*
Burnett, James A., 64

C
Caldwell, Molly, 33, 45*f*
Campfield, Harriette, 22
Carnegie, Andrew, 52
Carnegie Hall, 51–53, 53*f*
Caton, Herman L., 76
Central Congregational Church (West Newton, Massachusetts), 49
Chaffee, Mrs. Eugene W., 94–95

chapels, 50–51
Cheerful Workers Circle of the King's Daughters, 22
child marriages, 28–29
Chilhowee Mountain, 3, 8, 92
Circle of King's Daughters, 94
Clark, William Alonzo, 30–31
Clemens, Alice, 59
Click, Nell Jones, 109–110
Click, William D., 109–110
College Hill, 41, 42*f*
College Woods, 41, 43, 44*f*
Confederate army, 2
Co-operative Boarding Club, 52, 81
Corning, Mrs. Jasper, 56
Cox, James A., ix
Crawford, Gideon Stebbins White, 62
Crawford, Jennie Firdilla, 62
Crawford, Samuel Earle, 62–63
Croft, Mrs. Edward, 37
Cunningham, Ben, 41–42, 47
Cushman, Robert H., 25

D

Damiano, Charles, 97–98
Darling, William, 94
Daughters of the American Revolution
    chapter list of, 133–135
    donors from, 57–58, 95, 101
    Margaret Henry speaking to, 7
Dennis, Dora, 28–29
diseases, 46–47
donors, 133–135
Dorchester Daughters of Maine, 36
Douglas, Bertha, 22
Dudley, Mrs. R. D., 63
Dunn, Dolly, 14
Dunn, John, 13
Dunn, Will, 14
education rally, 57
Elizabeth Belcher Bullard Memorial Scholarship, 102

E

Elizabeth R. Voorhees Chapel, 50, 51*f*
Elmore, Edgar Alonzo, 61

F

February Meetings, 5, 139
Fenton, Mrs. Arthur P., 49
Forward Fund, 43, 52

G

General Federation of Women's Club, 73
Gibson, Mae, 33
Gibson, Otha Abraham, 88–89
gifts, 33–38
Gillingham, Alice, 42, 46, 49–51
Gillingham, Clinton, 49
Good Cheer Club, 23
Gustetter, F. C., 68, 91

H

Hagan, L. R., 95
Happy Valley Settlement School, 94
Henry, Bettie Jane, 121–122
Henry, Clemmie J. (cousin), ix–x, 70, 130
Henry, Cordelia, 99
Henry, Eliza Smith (mother), 2, 118, 137–138

Henry, Gray Smith (brother), 4–5, 138
Henry, John Smith (brother), 118
Henry, Lily, 31, 99–101
Henry, Margaret Eliza, xi*f*, 74*f*
- becoming scholarship secretary, 6–8, 140–142
- biographical sketch of, 137–147
- death of, 8–9, 137
- early life of, 4
- family of, 2–4
- funeral address of, 147–154
- gathering donors, 75–76, 142–143
- legacy of, 110–111, 145–146
- letters from, 11*f*, 39*f*, 71*f*, 105*f*
- love of children, 19–20
- on Maryville campus, 41–43
- memories of, 130–131
- missionary trip by, 140
- in Preparatory Department, 6
- and religious observations, 5, 139
- and Southern Mountains, 13–19
- success of, 143–144
- tombstone of, 119

Henry, Patrick, 143
Henry, Sarah (sister), 139
Henry, William Jasper, Jr. (brother), 4, 118
Henry, William Jasper, Sr. (father), 2, 118, 137
Henry, Zenie, 59
Home Economics Department (Maryville College), 56, 108
Hood, Robert N., 4
Hood, Sarah, 138
Hood, Sarah Mahala Henry, 8
Hopkins, Cora, 23–24
hospital, 46
Hotel Rutledge for Women, 8
Howell, Susan, 28
Hughes, William, 98–99
Hunter, Edwin Ray, 68–69, 68*f*
Hunter, Millie, 101–102
Hunter, Quinnie, 102

J

James, Cadelle, 86–88
James, Elijah Elihu, 86–88
Johnston, Nellie, 92–94
Jones, Mrs. George, 107, 109–110

K

Katonah Presbyterian Church, 61
Kenwood Evangelical Church of Chicago, 67
Kerr, Dr. and Mrs. J. T., 84
Kin Takahashi Week, ix, 113
Kinney, Sara T., 101
Kirkland, Hattie, 26–27
Kirkpatrick, Marivine, 107–108
Kirkpatrick, Nell Ross, 107–110, 108*f*

L

Lamar, Martha, 47
Lamar, Ralph Max, 47
Lamar, Thomas Jefferson, 47, 62
Lamar Memorial Hospital, 47–48, 47*f*
Lamar Memorial Library, 36
Lamb, Sarah E., 62
Lebar, Mrs. Frank, 68

Lee, Mr. and Mrs. Samuel McClung, 102
letters, from Margaret Henry, 11*f*, 39*f*, 71*f*, 105*f*
Lewis, Mr. and Mrs. Walter S., 24
Little Bald, 18–19
Livingstone, David, 3
Louis, Loudine, 110, 111*f*

M

MacDonald, Mrs. H. G., 21
MacLachlan, Isabel, 48–49
Magnolia Cemetery, 117–119
Margaret E. Henry Endowed Scholarship, 10, 111, 145
Maryville College, ix, 38*f*
- in 1903, 41
- buildings at, 46–55, 115–116
- College Hill, 42*f*
- College Woods, 41, 43, 44*f*
- education departments at, 55–58
- faculty of, 59–70
- hospital for, 46–48
- Margaret Eliza Henry legacy at, 8–9
- religious observations at, 49–51
- stream, 44*f*

Massachusetts State Federation of Women's Clubs, 92
May, Dori, ix
McBride, Robert, 2–4
McCampbell, Earl, 22–23
McClenaghan, S. J., 97
McCurry, Eula Erskine, 65–66, 65*f*
McMurray, Maude, 52
memorial funds, 146
Miles, Mary, 69–70
Miles, Thomas Judson, 69
Mills, Albert P., 54
missionary trips, 5–6, 95, 140
Moffat, Robert, 3, 140
Montvale Springs, 3
Moore, Hester, 127
Mori, Oki, 63
mountaineers, townspeople vs., 31–32

N

New Providence Presbyterian Church, 5, 9

O

"Old Dewberry" (ox), 80, 80*f*
Otis, Mr. and Mrs. Charles, 103

P

Parker, Mrs. John F., 60
Parks, Eleanor G., 29
Parsons, Mrs. John, 2
Patten, Elizabeth, 53*f*
Peacock, Mrs. Alexander, 48
Pearsons, Daniel K., 51–52
Pearsons Hall, 51–52, 52*f*
Peirce, Sara E., 36
Perkins, Angie Warren, 73–74, 76
Phillips, Nancy, 32–33
Pierson, H. Frank, 30
Porter, Francina E., 5–6, 140
Porter, Mrs. W. K., 60
Preparatory Department (Maryville College), 55–56
Presbyterian Board, 97
Princeton Sunday School, 34

Q

Quinby, Clara, 77

R

Reisner, Mrs. J. W., 66
religious observations, 5, 49–50
Roberts, Martha, 62
Robinson, Annie D., 48
Rogers, James, 5–6

S

Sanborn, Helen, 56
Sayer, Sarah. *See* Smith, Sarah (née Sayer)
scholarships, 7–8, 20–33, 75–76, 86–104
Scott, Mrs. George, 57
Scott Mountain, 14
Sisk, Augustus, 67*f*, 68
Smith, Belle, 123
Smith, James, 3
Smith, James Gray (maternal grandfather), 2–4, 117, 137, 139
Smith, Sarah (née Sayer; maternal aunt), 2–4, 117, 118, 138
Snyder, W. W., 61
Southern (Appalachian) Mountains, 13–39
  children of, 19–20, 21–23, 24
  gifts sent to, 33–38
  and Mae Swanner, 84–86
  scholarship recipients in, 20–33, 86–104
  and Stinnett family, 78–83
  travels through, 13–19
Spence's Cabin, 17
Stinnett, Colindy, 37
Stinnett, Dora, 78–81, 79*f*, 81*f*, 83
Stinnett, Granny, 123–125
Stinnett, Hobson, 24
Stinnett, Joe, 24
Stinnett, Lillie, 77–78, 80–81, 81*f*
Stinnett, Millie, 80–82
Stinnett, Moll, 78
Stinnett, Sallie Ann, 26, 41, 80–83
Stinnett cabin, 83*f*
Strong, Mrs. Frederick A., 75
Sudbury, Anne, 60
Swanner, Mae, 84–86
Sweetwater Valley, 128–130
swimming pool, 51, 54, 54*f*, 55*f*

T

Tabcat cabin, 109*f*
Teachers' Department (Maryville College), 58–59
Tennessee Historical Quarterly, 2
Tennessee State Federation of Women's Clubs, 8, 19, 76–77
Thunderhead, 13–14
townspeople, mountaineers vs., 31–32
Tucker Forge Farm, 103
Tullis, Flora Blanche, 128–130

V

Voorhees, Ralph, 50

W

Waite, Anne, 22
Walker, Arda Susan, 68
Walker, Black Bill, 76, 77*f*

Walker, Edgar Roy, 66*f*, 67–68
Walker, Julia, 89–90
Walker, Maggie L., 89–90
Walker, Nancy, 77*f*
Walker, Rufus, 89–91
Walker Valley, 20–22, 21*f*, 76–78, 125–128
Walker Valley School, 77, 78*f*
Wallace, William, 138
Waller, Elmer (dean), 6, 7*f*, 141, 147–148
Warren, Maude Battelle, 82
Webb, Gray, 4
Webster, Daniel, 4
Whetsell, Trissie, 57–58
Whitehead, Fred, 29–30
Wightman, Mrs. Percy, 26
Wilson, Rev. and Mrs. David M., 1
Wilson, Sam, 1, 5–6
Wilson, Samuel Tyndale, 6, 9–10, 9*f*, 42–46, 49, 56, 64
Winn, Alice D., 92
Winter, Elizabeth, 8, 145–146
Winter, Matilda, 8
Winter, Preston, 8
Women's Guild of North Presbyterian Church, 76
Woodhull, Mrs. J. R., 32
Woodruff, Edna, 35

Y

YMCA, 54

About the Author

Paula Cox Bowers has had strong ties with Maryville College all her life: when she was born in 1937, her father—who knew the value of a good education—registered her for the class of 1958; she entered the college in January 1956 as a biology major; and she also met her future husband, Rufus Bowers, at Maryville College. In 2006, Polly was part of a small group of volunteers who began reading and organizing the letters of Margaret Henry. Recognizing the treasure they had found, she decided to continue working regularly on Margaret's correspondence. Compiling and writing this book has been a labor of love.